Cambridge Elements ≡

Elements in Magic
edited by
Marion Gibson
University of Exeter

T0329138

THE *STRIX*-WITCH

Daniel Ogden
University of Exeter

CAMBRIDGE
UNIVERSITY PRESS

CAMBRIDGE
UNIVERSITY PRESS

University Printing House, Cambridge CB2 8BS, United Kingdom

One Liberty Plaza, 20th Floor, New York, NY 10006, USA

477 Williamstown Road, Port Melbourne, VIC 3207, Australia

314–321, 3rd Floor, Plot 3, Splendor Forum, Jasola District Centre, New Delhi – 110025, India

79 Anson Road, #06–04/06, Singapore 079906

Cambridge University Press is part of the University of Cambridge.

It furthers the University's mission by disseminating knowledge in the pursuit of education, learning, and research at the highest international levels of excellence.

www.cambridge.org
Information on this title: www.cambridge.org/9781108948821
DOI: 10.1017/9781108953474

© Daniel Ogden 2021

First published 2021

A catalogue record for this publication is available from the British Library.

ISBN 978-1-108-94882-1 Paperback
ISSN 2732-4087 (online)
ISSN 2732-4079 (print)

The *Strix*-Witch

Elements in Magic

DOI: 10.1017/9781108953474
First published online: May 2021

Daniel Ogden
University of Exeter
Author for correspondence: Daniel Ogden, d.ogden@ex.ac.uk

Abstract: The *strix* was a persistent feature of the folklore of the Roman world and subsequently that of the Latin West and the Greek East. She was a woman that flew by night, either in an owl-like form or in the form of a projected soul, in order to penetrate homes by surreptitious means and thereby devour, blight or steal the new-born babies within them. The motif-set of the ideal narrative of a *strix* attack – the '*strix*-paradigm' – is reconstructed from Ovid, Petronius, John Damascene and other sources, and the paradigm's impact is traced upon the typically gruesome representation of witches in Latin literature. The concept of the *strix* is contextualised against the longue-durée notion of the child-killing demon, which is found already in the ancient Near East, and shown to retain a currency still as informing the projection of the vampire in Victorian fiction.

Keywords: owl, vampire, soul-projection, motifs, witch

ISBNs: 9781108948821 (PB), 9781108953474 (OC)
ISSNs: 2732-4087 (online), 2732-4079 (print)

Contents

1 The Roman *Strix*: Terminology and Texts

1.1 The *Strix* Introduced

This *libellus* seeks to provide the tricky answer to an ostensibly simple question: What was a *strix*? Provisionally, let us say that she was a creature of the folklore of the Roman world and subsequently that of the Latin West and that of the Greek East. She was a woman that flew by night, either in a form akin to that of an owl or in the form of a projected soul, in order to penetrate homes by surreptitious means and thereby to devour, maim, blight or steal the new-born babies within them. The modern stereotype of the vampire is a reasonably close analogue.[1]

After a consideration of the Latin term, this section lays out the three most substantial accounts of the *strix* to survive – those in which she is explicitly so designated, at least – namely those of Ovid, Petronius and John Damascene.[2] This prepares the way for Section 2, the study's engine room. Here we analyse the recurring and constituent motifs of the *strix*'s modus operandi found in the three key texts and also, typically by way of passing allusions, in a substantial collection of further sources. From this we are able to reconstruct the ideal narrative of a *strix* attack – 'the *strix*-paradigm' – and it is this that enables us to offer a more complete and final answer to our fundamental question of what a *strix* was. Section 3 proceeds to demonstrate the profound impact of the *strix*-paradigm on the general representation of witches in the Latin literary tradition.[3] Section 4 looks at the *strix* in the context of a longue durée that starts with the child-killing demons of ancient Mesopotamia and ancient Greece and finishes with Gello, an active figure in modern Greek folklore as recently as the

---

[1] Recent work on *striges* has been dominated by the publications by Cherubini, most notably her monograph, 2010a (though much of the length is occupied with expansive excursuses on harpies, bears, the evil eye and theatrical masks), and 2010b (effectively a précis of the same in English); note also her 2009a and 2009b. Oliphant's pair of articles, 1913 and 1914, constitute the fundamental collation of the evidence. The material is discussed with some insight by McDonough 1997 and Spaeth 2010 (the latter focusing on the 'night hag'). Scobie 1978 provides wide-ranging folkloric comparanda (for which cf. also his 1983: 21–30 and Lawson 1910: 179–84). Beyond these items, see Boehm 1931, Curletto 1987, esp. 150–6, Gordon 1999: 204–10 (on the 'night-witch'), Touati 2003 (*non vidi*), Björklund 2017a, Hutton 2017: 67–72 ('the night-demoness').

[2] I do not touch here upon the focal argument developed in Ogden 2021, namely that, in addition to owls, *striges* may have had a secondary propensity to transform themselves into wolves – but I do begin my exposition here in the same way as I do there, by laying out the three key texts first, this being the clearest way to proceed.

[3] The semantic field of the term 'witch' includes the Latin literary creations discussed in Section 3 (which played their part in the English concept's development). The key term in Latin (by no means always expressed) is *venefica*; we shall encounter some of its synonyms, *saga*, *maga*, *cantatrix*.

turn of the twentieth century AD. This arms the pressing question as to whether there was specifically a Greek *strix* prior to the Latin one, or whether the Greek world effectively appropriated the Roman one. The Conclusion briefly addresses two further questions: Why did the *strix* matter to the ancients? And why does she matter to us?

All the major Classical and medieval sources for the *strix* are incorporated in translation.[4]

1.2 Terminology

The term *strix* signifies, in its simplest usage, a variety of owl. This is conventionally identified as the screech owl, for reasons that will become apparent, though some regard the term as indeterminate for species.[5] Often, however, and more pertinently to this study, it signifies a woman that flies by night to attack babies: sometimes she is imagined to take on the physical form of the owl, or a form with affinities to it, to accomplish this, but this was not always the case. The term appears in both Greek and Latin linguistic traditions in a dizzying range of variant forms. We cannot determine which of the two languages it originated in, nor, concomitantly, can we identify a secure etymology for it. We shall defer discussion of the Greek side to Section 4, but Table 1 offers the first attestations of the forms in which the word is found in the Latin tradition.[6]

Table 1 *Strix* terms in Latin: first attestations

Singular	Plural	Date of first attestation	Source of first attestation
strix	*striges/striges*	191 BC	Plautus *Pseudolus* 819–23
striga	*strigae*	c. AD 66	Petronius *Satyricon* 63
styx	**styges*	later ii AD	Hyginus *Fabulae* 28.4
stria	*striae*	AD 507–11	*Pactus legis Salicae* 64.3, *MGH Leges nat. Germ.* iv.1 p. 231

Note: A preceding asterisk (*) denotes a form that is not actually attested.

---

[4] Translations coinciding with my ancient-magic sourcebook (Ogden 2009) are taken over from it, with slight alterations.
[5] Cherubini 2009b: 77–8, 2010a: 21–5, 2010b: 65, 73–4 n.3 holds that the term was of broad usage and could designate any kind of owl, whilst contending that Ovid's description best suits a barn owl.
[6] Cf. LS and *OLD* s.vv.

The term is first attested in the third-declension form *strĭx* in Plautus' comedy *Pseudolus*, composed *c*. 200 BC, where it is associated with the devouring of human innards, and therefore refers to the woman as opposed to the simple bird. Petronius, who died in AD 66, deploys this same form in his novel, the *Satyricon*, but also a parallel first-declension form, *strīga*, this in a narrative given to the freedman Trimalchio (of which more anon). In both cases the word is applied to women again. Why the variation in form? Petronius works hard to characterise, indeed over-characterise, the language his uneducated, nouveau-riche freedmen speak, and so in placing the term *strīga* as he does in Trimalchio's mouth, he is telling us that this variant is déclassé – 'vulgar Latin', in both the informal and the formal senses. And, indeed, this *strix–striga* relationship crisply illustrates the broader tendency of Vulgar Latin to simplify third-declension nouns into first- or second-declension ones, which were more regular and predictable in terms of both grammar and gender.[7] As in many cases, vulgar terms represented the future of a language. In the Salic Law of AD 507–11, where once again the reference is to women, we accordingly find an evolved version of the *strīga* form, *stria* (the length of the *i* is unclear), which Gervase of Tilbury would later (AD 1209–14) classify as 'French'.[8] Despite this, one can imagine that the form *stria* may even have been in use already in Classical times, this under the influence of a similar word-group innocuously signifying 'furrow': *strĭx* (Vitruvius), *strĭga* (Columella) and *strĭa* (Varro). Ultimately, *strīga* evolved into the modern Italian *strega* ('witch'), a word familiar beyond Italy's borders for its use as the name of a mild herbal liqueur, its label suitably decorated with a broom-stick-toting figure.[9]

The form *styx* is probably erroneous. It is printed in editions of Hyginus' (later ii AD) *Fabulae*, including Marshall's Teubner version, where it seemingly denotes a pure bird, a distinctly sinister one that sits atop the column to which Otus and Ephialtes are forever bound, with snakes, in the underworld.[10] Hesychius specifies that the parallel Greek form signifies a little horned owl (*skōps*).[11] But what did Hyginus actually write? All editions of the *Fabulae* depend on the (inaccurate) first printed version of it made by Jacob Micyllus in 1535, after which the sole manuscript with which he worked was destroyed. By

[7] See above all Boyce 1991, esp. 49; for the language of Petronius' freedmen see also Blänsdorf 1990, Gaide 1995; for the term *striga* specifically see Ernout and Meillet 1959 s.v. *striga*, Väänänen 1967: 189–190, 232, Cherubini 2009a: 143, 2010a: 35, 2010b: 73 n.1. The ii AD grammarian Flavius Caper was still attempting to hold back the tide of vulgarity: *striges non strigae* (at Keil 1855–1923: vii.111, line 11).
[8] Gervase of Tilbury *Otia imperiala* 3.86.
[9] Cf. Oliphant 1913: 135, Cherubini 2009a: 143 n.2, 2010a: 14–16. [10] Hyginus *Fabulae* 28.
[11] Hesychius *s.v.* στύξ; however, there are complications with the Greek form in turn: see Section 4.3.

chance, two fragments of this manuscript, written in Benevantan script and dating to *c.* AD 900, have subsequently been discovered reused in book bindings, and are preserved in Munich. One of them contains the relevant portion of text, and we can now see that the scribe had originally written '*stri*' before correcting it to '*stys*'. It seems likely that the prior manuscript our *c.* AD 900 scribe had evidently struggled to decipher had read *strix*, and that the form *styx* did not, accordingly, exist in the Latin tradition.[12]

With *styx* cut from consideration, we may note that all variants of our term are first attested in the 'woman' sense as opposed to the 'pure-bird' sense.

1.3 Ovid's *Fasti*

Our starting-point in reconstructing the world of the *strix* must be a trio of paragraph-length texts all of which in their different ways offer rich and broadly synoptic accounts of the *strix* and her activities. Collectively, they permit us to reconstruct a basic paradigm for the phenomenon, as we proceed to do in the following section. Two of these are Latin texts from the Rome of the early empire, a passage from Ovid's *Fasti* and a passage from Petronius' *Satyricon*. The third is a Byzantine Greek passage of uncertain date and provenance, but which evidently draws ultimately on similar traditions. As we lay the passages out, we shall tag the tight set of related motifs emerging from them, in preparation for the analytical discussion that follows in Section 2.

The Augustan poet Ovid left his *Fasti* or *Calendar* unfinished when exiled by Augustus in AD 8. A didactic poem in elegiac couplets, it explains the origins of the Roman festivals and their associated customs. The 1st of June is sacred to the goddess Carna.[13] On this day sacrifices are offered to her in the grove of Alernus beside the Tiber. Ovid tells us that she had once been the nymph Cranae, a maiden-huntress in the style of Artemis-Diana. She had had a clever technique for maintaining her virginity. Whenever pressed by a suitor, she would invite him to lead the way to a discreet cave where they could make love, only to disappear into the bushes once his back was turned. The technique failed, however, when she caught Janus' eye, for the looking-both-ways god could of course see what happened behind him with the second face on the back of his head. In compensation for her defloration, he transformed her into Carna, the patron goddess of the door-hinge (*cardo*), and gave her the whitethorn or buckthorn as her sacred plant. With this she could defend doorways from supernatural attacks.[14] She was first called upon to use them to protect the little boy Proca, the future Alban king:

---

[12] See Marshall 2002: v–xiv, 43 (*ap. crit.*).　　[13] Ovid *Fasti* 6.101–30.
[14] The ancient hinge consisted of a pole running vertically down the side of the door, which rotated in sockets in the floor beneath and the lintel above.

[C] There are some rapacious birds. These are not the ones that cheated Phineus' mouth of his table [i.e., the Harpies], but they derive their descent from them. They have a large head, their eyes stand proud, their beaks are suited to snatching. There is greyness in their wings and there are hooks on their talons. [B] They fly by night [J] and seek out children without a nurse. [G] They snatch their bodies from their cradles and mar them. [H] They are said to tear apart the innards of suckling babies with their beaks, [I] and their throats are engorged with the blood they have drunk. [E] They are called *striges*; the reason for the name is that they are accustomed to screech [*stridere*] in dreadful fashion [B] during the night. Whether, then, these creatures are born in avian form, [A] or they are created by means of a spell, and a Marsian dirge transmutes old women into birds, [F] they came into Proca's bedchamber. The boy had been born just five days before, and now he was a fresh prey for them. [I] They sucked out his infant breast with eager tongues. The unfortunate child wailed and called for help. Alarmed at the cry of her charge, his nurse ran to him. She found that his cheeks had been gored by hard talons. What could she do? The colour of his face was that one sometimes finds in late leaves that have been damaged by the new frost. [N] She went to Carna and told her all. Carna said, 'There is no need to be frightened: your charge will be safe.' She came to the cradle. His mother and his father were weeping. 'Hold back your tears: I myself will heal him', she said. [F] At once she touched the doorposts, thrice over, with an arbutus branch, and three times she marked the threshold with her arbutus branch. She sprinkled the doorway with water (the water contained an infusion) [H] and she held the uncooked entrails of a two-month old sow [*porca*]. This is what she said: 'Birds of the night, spare the child's innards; for a small boy a small victim is sacrificed. I pray, take this heart for his heart, these liver-lobes for his liver-lobes. We give you this life to preserve a better one.'[15] When she had made her offering, she laid out the parts she had cut in the open air and forbade those attending the rite to look back at them. [F] A rod of Janus, taken from a whitethorn bush, was put where the small window allowed light into the bedchamber. It is said that after that the birds no longer invaded the cradle, and the boy's former colour returned to him.   Ovid *Fasti* 6.131–68[16]

It seems that the poet has confounded here the goddess Carna, whose province was in fact, suitably enough, the protection of flesh (*caro*, *carnis*), with another goddess, Cardea, whose province was indeed the protection of the hinge (*cardo*).[17] In glossing Ovid, the v AD antiquarian Macrobius affirms that the goddess Carna's province had consisted of internal organs such as livers and hearts.[18] But the

---

[15] I.e., a *porca* is given in substitution for *Proca*: see McDonough 1997: 333, Spaeth 2010: 243–4.
[16] For exegesis of this passage see Oliphant 1913: 140–3, Frazer 1929: iv, 141–4, Bömer 1958–63: ii, 344–5, Scobie 1978: 76, Littlewood 2006: 45–51, Cherubini 2010a: 25–34, 2010b: 66–7.
[17] See Frazer 1929: iv, 141–2.
[18] Macrobius *Saturnalia* 1.12.32; however, it may be that he had no other source than Ovid upon which to rely, as McDonough 1997: 328–30 notes. See also Pettazzoni 1940: 164, and Cherubini 2010b: 67.

conflation, whether originating with Ovid or otherwise, is probably a deliberate and knowing one, given that the goddess that defends against *striges* must protect both bodily organs – flesh – and doorways alike.

1.4 Petronius' *Satyricon*

Petronius Arbiter left behind his once massive comic novel, the *Satyricon*, when executed by Nero, *c.* AD 66.[19] The main surviving portion of the work describes an outrageously tasteless dinner party hosted by the nouveau-riche freedman Trimalchio, and in the course of this a pair of lurid stories are exchanged between the host and his fellow freedman Niceros. Niceros begins by telling a werewolf story (of which more anon) and Trimalchio responds to it with the following tale:

> [N] I myself will tell you a tale to make you shudder: an ass upon the roof-tiles. When I still had my hair long (for from being a boy I led a life of 'Chian' luxury), our master's favourite boy died. He was a pearl, and delightful in every respect. While his pitiful mother was mourning over him, and many of us were feeling miserable about it, [E] the *strigae* suddenly started to screech [*stridere*].[20] You would have thought it was a dog chasing a hare. We had at that time a Cappadocian slave, tall, quite daring, and strong. [F] He boldly drew his sword and ran out of the door, carefully binding up his left hand to use as a shield. He ran one of the women through, in the middle, round about here – gods preserve the part of my body I indicate. [D] We heard a groan, but – honestly, I won't lie – we did not actually see them. Our great hulk of a man returned within and threw himself down on the bed. [H] His whole body was black and blue, as if he'd been beaten with whips (this was obviously because an evil hand [*mala manus*] had touched him). [F] We shut the door and returned to what we were doing, but, when the mother embraced the body of her son, as she touched it she realized that it was just a tiny thing made of straw. [H] It had no heart or guts, nothing. [D, G] You see, the *strigae* had stolen the boy and left a straw doll in his place. I beg you to believe it.[21] [A] Women that know something more [*plussciae*] do exist, [B] night-women [*nocturnae*] do exist, and what is up, they can make down.[22] But that hulking man never properly recovered his colour after this adventure, and indeed he went mad and died a few days later.   Petronius *Satyricon* 63[23]

---

[19] Rose 1971 articulates the standard approach to the problems of the work's date and authorship.
[20] The manuscript is corrupt at this point; this key term has – very plausibly – been restored by editors.
[21] See Section 2.4 for the justification of the identification of Motif D here.
[22] A reference in the first instance, perhaps, to the propensity of ancient witches to draw down the moon, as, e.g., at Horace *Epodes* 5.46, Lucan *Pharsalia* 6.500–6 and Petronius *Satyricon* 134; cf. Hill 1973.
[23] For exegesis of this passage see Cherubini 2010a: 34–41, Schmeling 2011: 260–4.

Although nothing is said of it, it is possible that we are to imagine that the women have been responsible for the boy's death in the first place.[24]

1.5 A Byzantine Fragment: John Damascene?

The seemingly long-lived John of Damascus (*c.* AD 650–*c.* AD 750) was an Arab Christian and the author over thirty philosophical and polemical works, largely compilatory in style. It is his misfortune that the work for which he is best known, the romance *Barlaam and Ioasaph*, was written by somebody else. Similarly transmitted as his, but not necessarily by his hand, is a homiletic fragment classified under the title *De draconibus et strygibus*, 'On dragons and striges'.[25] There seems to be no particular bond between the treatments of the two topics, and it may be that the text comprises two separate fragments rather than one. It has been contended that the material bearing upon dragons at any rate was written by the ninth-century AD Kekaumenos, author of the *Stratēgikon*.[26] However, the material on *striges*, whenever it was penned and whatever its age and provenance, seemingly has deep and ancient roots, given the degree of the integration of its motifs with the two passages laid out so far, as well as with the other ancient texts we shall consider in the following two sections. It reads as follows:

I don't want you to be ignorant about this. [N] Some less well-educated people say that there are women called *stryngai* and also *geloudes*. [B, D] They say that they appear through the air by night. [F] Arriving at a house, they find no hindrance in doors and bolts, but get in even when doors have been securely locked, and smother the children. [H] Others say that they devour their liver [I] and all their moisture [K] and impose a time-limit on their lives. Some insist that they have seen them, [D, E] others that they have heard them. [F] Somehow, they enter houses, even though the doors have been locked, together with their body, [D] or just by means of their bare soul. And I will declare that only Christ, Jesus Christ our God, was able to do this. After he rose again from the dead, he entered through locked doors to meet his holy apostles. [A] But if a woman mage did this, and does it, then the Lord no longer did anything amazing with the locked doors. [D] If they were to say that she enters the house just as a bare soul, with her body resting on a bed, then hear what I have to say, which is what our Lord Jesus Christ said: 'I have the power to lay down my soul, and I have the power in myself to take it up

---

[24] Cf. the XV AD evidence (from Kieckhefer 1998) adduced in Sections 2.17 and 3.1, where *strix*-like witches are said to penetrate houses magically in order to blight and kill the children within and then, in a second action, retrieve their bodies after burial for consumption or magical exploitation.

[25] It is branded as 'dubious' in Geerard's *Clavis patrum Graecorum*: *CPG* 8087, Fragmenta 1 and 2.

[26] Litavrin 2003: 636–43.

again.'[27] And he did this once on the occasion of his holy passion. [A] But if
a disgusting woman mage can do this whenever she wishes, then the Lord did
nothing more than what she does. [H] And if she has devoured the child's
liver, how is he able to live? [N] All this is nonsense talked by some heretics
opposed to the one and holy Church, with a view to diverting some people of
the simpler sort from orthodoxy.

John Damascene *On Dragons and Witches, PG* 94,1604[28]

Any doubts that the ideas enshrined in this rather later text belong closely
with those of the Ovid and Petronius texts should be assuaged by the end of
Section 3.

2 The Motif-Set and Paradigm

In this, the pivotal section, we analyse the overlapping network of motifs
associated with the *striges* in the (predominantly) Latin tradition of the ancient
and medieval eras, and reconstruct an ideal narrative of a *strix* attack. This
project is rendered feasible by the fundamental coherence, consistency and
conservatism of *strix* lore throughout, and it is upon this enduring core of belief
that we focus our attention, rather than attempting to pursue the particularities of
the handlings of *strix* imagery in individual authors, or nuanced shifts in the
significance of the *strix* as she passed from one age to another or from the
context of one broader belief-system to that of another.

2.1 Motif A: The *Strix* as an (Old) Witch

That the *striges* are conceptualised as witches is explicit in Ovid's text, where it
is said that – by one hypothesis – old women transform themselves into the
aviform creatures in question by means of a spell or a 'Marsian dirge'. Here
'Marsian' is a metonymy for 'magical'. The Romans ever associated the Marsi
of Marruvium, on the shore of Lake Fucinus, with magic, and in particular with
the charming and bursting open of snakes.[29] The Romans typically conceptualised witches in general – as we still do – as old women: Horace's Canidia ('Grey
One') wears false teeth, whereas her companion Sagana ('Wise One') sports
a wig;[30] when Apuleius' Meroe complains that her former lover Socrates has
mocked her youthful innocence, it is with no little irony[31] (these figures will be
considered in more detail later: 3.1, 3.5).

The classification of the *striges* as witches is more or less explicit in
Petronius' text too, where the story narrated is presented in affirmation of the

---

[27] John 10:18.   [28] Translation taken over from Ogden 2018.
[29] See Letta 1972, esp. 139–45, Tupet 1976: 187–98, Dench 1995: 159–66.
[30] Horace *Satires* 1.8.48–50.   [31] Apuleius *Metamorphoses* 1.12.

truth that 'Women that know something more do exist.' The term 'knowing something more', *plus-sciae*, is suggestive both of the esoteric knowledge of witchcraft and also of age and experience.[32]

John Damascene's Greek text designates its *strix* by the slightly paradoxical phrase 'woman mage' (*magos . . . gynē*), a 'mage' being inherently male. It is curious that this phrase should be used in place of the standard Greek term for 'witch', *pharmakis*, which originally described a female manipulator of herbs or spells, *pharmaka*.[33] The same designation is also found in a fable of Aesop's preserved in a Byzantine collection, where a 'woman mage' (*gynē magos*), who has claimed to be able to placate the anger of the gods, is condemned for religious innovation and taken off for execution.[34] As often with the Aesopic fables, it is difficult to know how old this tale actually is, but it must post-date the turn of the fourth century BC at any rate. Religious innovation was famously one of the two crimes that led to Socrates' execution in 399 BC.[35] But the fable may even belong in its entirety to the Byzantine age, to which, indeed, the phrase 'woman mage' may be confined. Perhaps the phrase originated in an attempt to forge an equivalent to the appropriately feminised Latin term *maga*, first attested in one of the younger Seneca's plays (before AD 65), where it is applied to women making love potions; it is subsequently applied by Augustine to Circe as she transforms Odysseus' companions into pigs in his AD 426 *City of God*.[36]

A bilingual glossary, the *Glossary of Philoxenus*, preserved solely in a ix AD manuscript, offers the following Greek gloss on the Latin form *striga*: 'a Laestrygonian, and a witch woman [*gynē pharmakis*]'.[37]

2.2 Motif B: Operating by Night

For Ovid the *striges* 'fly by night and seek out children without a nurse'. John Damascene observes that 'They say that they appear through the air by night.' But it is Petronius' text that is the most valuable here. His Trimalchio does not initially identify the time at which the action of his tale takes place, but, when he draws his conclusion, he presents his tale as an affirmation of the truth not only that 'women that know something more do exist' but also that 'night-women

---

[32] *Plussciae*, as a single word, would be a *hapax*; see Schmeling 2011 *ad loc.* and Cherubini 2010a: 167–8 n.168 for justification of it; but perhaps we should read, more simply, *plus sciae* ('knowledgeable in respect of more').

[33] For ancient herbal magic see now Watson 2019: 116–47.

[34] Aesop *Fables* 56 Perry. The tale is preserved in the xvi AD manuscript (codex Laurentianus 57.30) of a fable-collection made by the later xiii AD Maximus Planudes.

[35] Plato *Apology* 24b–c.   [36] Seneca *Hercules Oetaeus* 523; Augustine *City of God* 18.17.

[37] *Glossary of Philoxenus* s.v. *striga*; for the text see Laistner 1926. The glossary is partly derivative of Festus. We shall discuss the significance of 'Laestrygonian' in Section 4.

[*nocturnae*] do exist'. We infer, accordingly, that it is not merely the case that *striges* contingently tend to operate by night; rather, night-time activity lies at the heart of their identity.

Further references to the *strix* as a nocturnal creature abound, although in most cases they seem to refer to the pure owl in the first instance, which, obviously, was nocturnal in its own right.[38] One more text is worthy of particular mention, however: the ii AD medical poet Quintus Serenus Sammonicus speaks of a 'black' *strix* attacking boys with her 'fetid dugs' (the full text is quoted in Section 2.10). I take the adjective 'black' here to be a transferred epithet saluting the night-time circumstances in which she works.[39]

2.3 Motif C: Flying and Bird Transformation

The *strix* flies by night to do her work – but how? There are two rather distinct models. According to the first, the *strix* transforms herself into an owl or an owl-like entity to make her attack, as we shall discuss in this section. According to the second, she projects her soul from her body to do her work for her, invisibly, but somehow tangibly, as we shall discuss in Section 2.4.

It seems unlikely that the creature responsible for the child-attacking phenomenon with which we are concerned was ever conceived of as the simple bird *tout court*. Rather, the child-attacking *strix* always seems to have been conceived of as a woman first, a woman capable of transforming herself into a bird, or a woman with avian elements or abilities, not least the ability to fly. There is no explicit reference to birds at all – except insofar as it might be considered inherent in the word *strix* itself – in our key passages of Petronius and John Damascene, for whom the creatures are clearly first and foremost women. In a fragment of (the i BC) Verrius preserved by (the later ii AD) Festus *striges* are again apparently understood first and foremost as 'flying women', albeit the protective Greek charm he then quotes seems in itself to speak only of pure birds:

---

[38] At Horace *Epodes* 5.15–24 (*c.* 30 BC) the horrid witch Canidia uses 'a feather of the nocturnal *strix*' alongside other unpleasant ingredients in a love potion. At Lucan *Pharsalia* 6.689 (AD 65) the disturbing blend of animal noises the super-witch Erictho produces as part of her spell to retrieve a dead soul from the underworld and compel it to reanimate its parent corpse include 'the complaints of the eagle-owl [*bubo*], the complaints of the nocturnal *strix*'. An ill omen at Statius' *Thebaid* 3.511 (*c.* AD 91) includes 'nocturnal *striges*'. The Damigeron-Evax *Lapidary*, a v–vi AD Latin adaptation of a lost Hellenistic Greek original, prescribes the manufacture of an amulet against *nyktalōpes*, literally, 'creatures that see by night', and then glosses the term with the phrase, 'which is to say, against nocturnal birds [*nocturnae aves*], i.e., *striges* or tawny owls [*cavanae*]' (28.1); Halleux and Schamp 1985: 266–7 and Cherubini 2009b: 80 n.8, 2010a: 158 n.62 contend that this phrase of explanation is a late interpolation. Isidore of Seville *Etymologies* 12.7.42 (early vii AD) refers briefly to 'the *strix*, the nocturnal bird'.

[39] Quintus Serenus Sammonicus *Liber medicinalis* 58, ll. 1029–38.

As Verrius says, the Greeks call a *strix* [Lat.] a *strinx* [Gk.] ... the name is applied to evil-doing women, whom they also call 'flying women' [*volaticae*]. And so the Greeks have the custom of, as it were, averting them with these words: '[Gk.] Send away the *strinx*, the long-eared-owl-*strinx*,[40] from people, the bird that should not be named, onto swift-faring ships [sc. to carry her away to a desolate place where she can do no harm].'

Festus p. 414 Lindsay = PMG 858[41]

Of our three principal authors, it is Ovid that comes closest to suggesting that child-attacking *striges* may sometimes have been pure birds,[42] in supplying a detailed description: 'They have a large head, their eyes stand proud, their beaks are suited to snatching. There is greyness in their wings and there are hooks on their talons ... They are said to tear apart the innards of suckling babies with their beaks ....' However, the notion of avian purity is challenged both by his initial introduction of the creatures as descended from the Harpies and by his subsequent qualification: 'Whether, then, these creatures are born in avian form, or they are created by means of a spell, and a Marsian dirge transmutes old women into birds ....'[43]

Much of the mythology of the Harpies (*Harpyiai*, 'Snatchers') makes them a good fit as ancestors of the *striges*.[44] Originally conceptualised as storm-winds, as is directly indicated by their alternative collective name, Thyellai, and by some of their individual 'speaking' names, Aello, Aellopous,[45] their characteristic activity in the *Odyssey* is to carry off, not food, as in their famous appearance in the tale of Phineus,[46] but people, never to be seen again. Such they did to the daughters of Pandareus,[47] and such they are imagined to have done to the missing Odysseus.[48] Already in Hesiod, however, and then in Aeschylus, they are conceptualised rather as flying, winged maidens.[49] In later texts they are given a more evolved form. Virgil describes them as follows:

---

[40] 'Long-eared-owl': *nyktiboa*.

[41] Unfortunately, the texts both of Verrius' own words and of the Greek charm he quoted are dreadfully corrupt (for a sobering printing of the text as transmitted, see Cherubini 2010a: 153–4 n.11), but this seems to be the gist.

[42] Isidore of Seville *Etymologies* 12.7.42 also comes close: he refers to child-attacking *striges* as birds, but in going on to assert that they give suck to babies, he reveals that the creature he has in mind is not purely avian; for text and further discussion see Section 2.10.

[43] *Striges* and Harpies are compared also at Silius Italicus *Punica* 13.598.

[44] For an expansive comparison of the two creatures see Cherubini 2010a: 53–75, a major part of her thesis.

[45] Homer *Odyssey* 20.61–77, Hesiod *Theogony* 265–9, Hyginus *Fabulae* 14.

[46] Aeschylus *Eumenides* 50–1 and F258 *TrGF*, Apollonius Rhodius *Argonautica* 2.179–434, Valerius Flaccus *Argonautica* 4.423–528, Statius *Thebaid* 8.255–8, Apollodorus *Bibliotheca* 1.121–3, Hyginus *Fabulae* 19, Apuleius *Metamorphoses* 10.15, Oppian *Cynegetica* 2.612–28.

[47] Homer *Odyssey* 20.61–77. [48] Homer *Odyssey* 1.241, 14.371.

[49] Hesiod *Theogony* 265–9; cf. Aeschylus *Eumenides* 50–1.

'Birds with the countenances of girls ... their hands are curved into talons, their faces ever pallid with hunger.'[50] And Hyginus: 'These are said to have been feathered, to have had cocks' heads, wings, human arms, cocks' feet with huge talons, and the breasts and belly of a human woman.'[51] Tzetzes' (xii AD) notes that the bottom half of a Harpy is that of a bird.[52] In ancient art Harpies are usually shown simply as winged maidens, though they can occasionally – whilst retaining their humanoid upper torsos and arms – also acquire bird-tails and bird-legs.[53]

In his *Metamorphoses* (completed by AD 8) Ovid includes the following amongst the terrible – and in some cases impossible – ingredients Medea blends in her cauldron to make a magical rejuvenating brew with which to suffuse the limbs of Jason's aged father Aeson:

> She added frosts collected under the all-night moon, the notorious wings of the *strix*, together with its flesh, and the entrails of the shape-shifting wolf, which changes its wild-animal form into a man.
>
> Ovid Metamorphoses 7.268–71

Whilst the reference may initially seem to speak of the pure bird, the creature's collocation in the list with the werewolf rather invites us to suppose that the bird in question is a woman transformed, just as a werewolf is a man transformed.

Pliny has the following words on the *strix*, from a natural-historical perspective:

> The only female creatures to have nipples on their breast are those that are able to nurse their offspring. None of the creatures that lays eggs has nipples, and only those that give birth to live young have milk. The bat [*vespertilio*] is the only bird that has milk.[54] For I consider the claim made of *striges*, that they milk their dugs into the lips of babies, to belong to the realm of stories [*fabulosum*]. It is accepted that the *strix* has long existed in the realm of curses, but I do not believe it to be established what bird it is [*or*: whether it is a bird].[55]   Pliny *Natural History* 11.232[56]

---

50 Virgil *Aeneid* 3.216–18. For the possibility that Ovid's description of the *striges* is specifically derived from Virgil's description of the Harpies here, see Bömer 1958–63: ii, 344–5 and Scobie 1978: 76.

51 Hyginus *Fabulae* 14. They are specifically birdlike also at Ovid *Metamorphoses* 7.4, Seneca *Hercules Furens* 759, *Medea* 781–2, Valerius Flaccus *Argonautica* 4.494, 498 (*stridunt alae* – 'their wings screech'), Statius *Thebaid* 8.255–8 (*stridere*), Oppian *Cynegetica* 2.620.

52 Tzetzes on Lycophron *Alexandra* 653.

53 See *LIMC* Harpyiai, esp. no. 5 (Pompeian mosaic, Naples, Museo Nazionale 9981), with Kahil 1988.

54 For the ancients' understandable tendency to classify the bat as a bird (or at any rate with birds), see the evidence collected at Oliphant 1913: 134 n.4.

55 *sed quae sit avium, constare non arbitror.*   56 For discussion, see Cherubini 2010a: 23.

Pliny is sceptical all round, but he virtually asserts here that if *striges* do indeed force their milk into babies' mouths, then they cannot be pure birds. The weak implication is then that they are either humanoid (by default), or semi-humanoid.

In commenting on the physical form of the *strix*, McDonough notes Pliny's 'confessed uncertainty', and maintains: 'it seems best to consider the *strix* as undefinable, composed of the parts of many fearful animals but identified with no particular one: it is ... a creature "betwixt and between."'[57] 'Betwixt and between', perhaps, but there is no reason to suppose that the *strix* ever boasted body parts other than those of a woman or an owl.

2.4 Motif D: Flying and Soul-Projection – Invisibility

For Petronius' Trimalchio and John Damascene *striges* make their attack not in the form of a bird or bird-like creature, but rather invisibly – though it is not excluded that they make their attack in the form of an invisible bird-like creature. In Trimalchio's narrative no one sees the terrible witches that surround and besiege the house in question. Even when the Cappadocian slave succeeds in running one of them through, we are told: 'We heard a groan, but – honestly, I won't lie – we did not actually see them.' And we are left to infer by the clues Petronius allows Trimalchio to leave in his story that the method by which they were able to enter and exit the house again was by passing through its door invisibly when it was opened, first for the Cappadocian to run out against them (the screeching was no doubt designed to lure him into doing so), and then when it was opened again to receive the blighted slave upon his return.

What sort of invisibility is this? The achievement of invisibility is a common enough feat in the ancient magical repertoire. We hear, for example, of rings that can confer it.[58] And we might think also of the 'husband-blinding' spells with which witches help women to commit adultery: the spells do not literally blind the husband, merely render him incapable of recognising what is going on under his nose.[59] But the John Damascene text directs us to look for a different sort of invisibility: 'Somehow they enter houses, even though the doors have been locked, together with their body, or just by means of their bare soul ... a witch enters the house just as a bare soul, with her body resting on a bed.' The second alternative noted is soul-flight, the phenomenon by which an individual is able to separate their soul from their

---

[57] McDonough 1997: 326.

[58] Plato *Republic* 359d–60b (the ring of Gyges), *Cyranides* 1.15.33–7; cf. *PGM* I.222–32 (an invisibility lotion).

[59] Tibullus 1.2.42–66, Propertius 4.5.15.

body, which is left in a catatonic state, and send it off on journeys of its own, or even, as must be entailed here, somehow or other to engage semi-tangibly with the world around it. It is implied that a wispy detached soul can squeeze its way into the house – invisibly, presumably – through a hinge-gap, or a crack in the wall, of both of which more anon, or perhaps even through a keyhole.

Compatibly with broader *strix* imagery, detached souls were often conceived of as aviform in the ancient world. For both Homer and Virgil the crowding ghosts of the underworld resemble flocks of birds, whilst for Sophocles a soul quits the body in the form of a 'fair-winged bird'.[60] In Archaic and Classical Greek art, soul-birds can be seen to hover over dead bodies, or perch upon them.[61] On the *lekythoi* (little oil flasks) of these eras too, detached souls are often depicted as tiny flying creatures resembling vertically hovering dragon-flies: it is easy to imagine such creatures passing through the tiniest cracks of a house.[62]

But the *locus classicus* for soul-flying in the Classical world is the collection of anecdotes attaching to a group of mythical figures in the Pythagorean tradition, who, by the imperial age at any rate, had come to be regarded as wizards.[63] Strabo, writing under Tiberius, considers the most prominent of these, Aristeas of Proconnesus, to constitute the prime example of a wizard, if ever there was one.[64] Let us look briefly at three characters in this tradition. The nature of their activity is most succinctly conveyed by the tale that the (ii BC) paradoxographer Apollonius tells of Hermotimus of Clazomenae:

> The following sort of thing is reported of Hermotimus of Clazomenae. They say his soul would wander from his body and stay away for many years. Visiting places, it would predict what was going to happen, for example torrential rains or droughts, and in addition earthquakes and pestilences and the suchlike. His body would just lie there, and after an interval his soul would return to it, as if to its shell, and arouse it. He did this frequently, and whenever he was about to go on his travels he gave his wife the order that no one, citizen or anyone, should touch his body. But some people came into the house, prevailed upon his wife and observed Hermotimus lying on the floor naked and motionless. They brought fire and burned him, in the belief that, when the soul came back and no longer had anything to re-enter, he would be completely deprived of life. This is exactly what happened. The people of

---

[60] Homer *Odyssey* 11.605–6, Virgil *Aeneid* 6.310–12; Sophocles *Oedipus Tyrannus* 175.
[61] For these see Haavio 1958, Curletto 1987.
[62] E.g., *LIMC* Charon 1 nos. 1–3. For more on the phenomena mentioned in this paragraph, see Ogden 2001: 221–4.
[63] For these figures ('the Greek shamans') see Bolton 1962, Burkert 1962, 1972: 140–65, Bremmer 2016, Ustinova 2009, esp. 47–51.
[64] Strabo C589: ἀνὴρ γόης, εἴ τις ἄλλος.

Clazomenae honour Hermotimus even to this day and have a temple to him. Women may not enter it for the reason above [i.e., the wife's betrayal].

Apollonius *Historiae Mirabiles* 3

The richest suite of stories is associated with Aristeas himself, with Herodotus already having much to say of him in the later fifth century BC, albeit in a somewhat confused fashion.[65] The (ii AD) Maximus of Tyre offers a more pointed summary:

> The body of a man of Proconnesus would lie there breathing, albeit indistinctly and in a fashion close to death. His soul would escape from his body and wander through the ether like a bird, observing everything beneath, land, sea, rivers, cities, peoples, their experiences and the natural world. Then it would enter into his body again and set it back on its feet, as if it were making use of an instrument, and it would recount the various things it had seen and heard among the various peoples.   Maximus of Tyre 10.2

The most resonant detail in this summary for us, in this context, is the claim that 'His soul would escape from his body and wander through the ether like a bird.' We find it in a more specific form elsewhere: Pliny tells that Aristeas' soul could be seen to fly forth out of his catatonic mouth in the form of a raven.[66] Interesting here too are the words of (the iii AD) Porphyry on another of these Pythagorean figures, Abaris the Hyperborean:

> Abaris acquired the title 'air-traveler', because he rode on an arrow given him by Hyperborean Apollo and crossed rivers and seas and inaccessible places, travelling somehow through the air. Some supposed that Pythagoras had exercised the same power when he conversed with his companions in both Metapontum and Tauromenium on the same day.
>
> Porphyry *Life of Pythagoras* 28–9

Here soul-flying is expressed through the imagery of flying on an arrow – a feathered object. These texts allow us, by analogy, partially to bridge the dichotomy between the accounts of the *striges* in which they fly as birds and those in which they fly as souls.

It is likely that *striges* were most commonly imagined to carry out their work invisibly. The point will come home more forcefully when we come to consider also the motif of the *striges*' damaging of the body from within by surreptitious or invisible means (Section 2.10, Motif J).

2.5 Motif E: Screeching

We have noted that the word *strix* has no (real) etymology. But it did enjoy a thriving folk-etymology in the Latin tradition, where it is often associated,

---

[65] Herodotus 4.13–16.   [66] Pliny *Natural History* 7.174.

appropriately enough, with the verb *strīdēre* and the corresponding noun *strīdŏr*, both 'screech', either explicitly or implicitly.[67] Screeching is central to Ovid's conceptualisation of the *strix*: 'They are called *striges*; the reason for the name is that they are accustomed to screech [*stridere*] in dreadful fashion during the night.'[68] The etymology was doubtless older than Ovid, and it long survived him. In the early seventh century AD Isidore of Seville repeated that 'The *strix* ... takes its name from the sound of its voice; for its call is a screech.'[69]

Petronius almost certainly offers the same folk-etymology, albeit in slightly subtler fashion: 'the *strigae* suddenly started to screech [*stridere*]. You would have thought it was a dog chasing a hare.'[70] His text is corrupt at the key point here, and *stridere* is an editorial restoration, but a near-certain one: at any rate the *striges* have to be making some sort of terrible noise outside the house to draw the Cappadocian out, so that they can infiltrate it as he opens the door. And indeed this screeching – if that is what it is – is accordingly pivotal to the story.

The 'screech' might be thought to belong particularly to the avian *strix*, but it rather comes into its own in the cases of attacks by invisible *striges*. As Petronius' Trimalchio says, 'We heard a groan, but – honestly, I won't lie – we did not actually see them.' And as John Damascene notes, 'Some insist that they have seen them, others that they have [*sc.* only] heard them.' After all, how else, other than by sound, is one to detect the presence of the invisible *striges*? How else is one to dread their attack? Indeed, it is a commonplace of a number of mysterious phenomena in the ancient world that they should be heard but not seen. Lucian's animated statue of Pellichus, which is said get off its pedestal and wander around Eucrates' villa by night, is heard in its nocturnal activities, but sometimes not seen in them: 'Indeed, he often bathes and plays around all through the night, with the result that one can hear the splashing of the water.'[71] Of Pellichus, more anon (Section 2.10).

The cry of the *strix* may perhaps be considered to have a magical effect in itself. Lucan's witch Erictho prefaces the reanimation spell with which she will restore a dead Pompeian soldier to life for necromantic purposes with an inarticulate cry: 'The voice contained the barking of dogs and the howling of wolves, the complaining cries of a scared eagle-owl [*bubo*] and the night's *strix*, the screeching and bellowing of wild animals, and the hissing of the snake.'[72]

---

[67] For the perceived relationship between *strix* and *stridere* see Curletto 1987: 151, Maltby 1990: 586–7, Cherubini 2010a: 9–21.
[68] Ovid *Fasti* 6.139–40.   [69] Isidore of Seville *Etymologies* 12.7.42.
[70] Petronius *Satyricon* 63.   [71] Lucian *Philopseudes* 19; see the discussion at Ogden 2007: 143.
[72] Lucan *Pharsalia* 6.685–90.

2.6 Motif F: Imperceptibility and the Battle of the House

The battle between the *strix* and the child's protective parents takes place above all at the point of the house's outer shell or boundary. As I have observed before, 'The challenge for the *striges* is to penetrate this boundary; the challenge for the householders is to keep it secure, with doors and windows constituting particular points of vulnerability.'[73] The battle of the house is saluted in our three principal authors, each of whom conceptualises it in a different way.

Ovid's Carna, in gestures with a long aetiological significance for Roman custom, seeks to protect the doorways of Proca's house against attack from the *striges* by brushing them with the arbutus branch and by sprinkling them with water, whilst defending the windows with a rod made from a whitethorn bush. This rather suggests that a door or window may be open, or afford small openings even when shut, but remain protected by the virtue of the magical plants brought into contact with them.

The logic of the narrative Petronius gives to Trimalchio is rather different. It would seem here, by default, that a simple door, tightly fitting or otherwise, is proof against penetration by the *striges*, just so long as it does actually remain shut whilst the women are on the prowl. In this case the challenge for the *strix* is to trick the householder into opening the door, however briefly, to let her in, and then she is able to pass through it invisibly and unperceived. In Trimalchio's tale, as we have noted, the witches trick the Cappadocian slave into opening the door so as to be able to rush out and attack the householders, by means of the activity at the heart of their identity, screeching (Motifs D, E, F).

But such a simple protection would not have been good enough against John Damascene's *striges*, who, as we have seen, are evidently able to pass through tiny apertures – hinge-gaps, cracks in the wall – by means of projecting their souls into wispy, flying entities. Inevitably, this means of penetration is also imperceptible – or visually imperceptible at any rate. Once again, we note the phrase, 'Some insist that they have seen them, others that they have [*sc.* only] heard them.' No doubt John's introductory phrase, 'Arriving at a house, they find no hindrance in doors and bolts, but get in even when doors have been securely locked', is intended tendentiously nonetheless: locked doors do indeed remain a hindrance, and a challenge to be overcome, but a challenge to which the *strix* is capable of rising with her special powers. Against such powers of entry, presumably only magical means of protection will suffice, plant-based or other.[74]

---

[73] Ogden 2021: 33.

[74] It is not to be excluded that John Damascene's *strix* can travel, in soul form, not merely through tiny apertures in doors (and presumably windows) but also through the substance of the solid doors themselves. We recall that at Homer *Odyssey* 11.204–8 the ghost of Odysseus' mother passes through his solid arms when he tries to embrace her.

What is entailed by John's phrase, 'Somehow they enter houses, even though the doors have been locked, together with their body, or just by means of their bare soul'? Does John also envisage that a *strix* – perhaps one in the form of a bruising, sharp-beaked, sharp-clawed bird – can enter a house by simple physical means? Possibly, but the phrase may be addressed more to the uncertainty that must attend the *strix*'s physical status once she has successfully penetrated the house in projected-soul form. If she is to proceed to harm the baby, even just smother it (as John specifies), then she surely needs a degree of physicality or solidity once within. The conundrum goes unresolved – perhaps significantly and creatively so. It is a conundrum that attends sinister tales of detached souls of other kinds in the ancient world – permanently detached ones, i.e., ghosts. In his (later ii AD) *Metamorphoses* Apuleius, for example, tells the tale of a disaffected wife who hires 'some old crone, who was held to be able to accomplish absolutely anything through binding curses and witchcraft [*maleficiis*]', to kill her husband, a miller. The witch sends a ghost to do the job:

> At around the middle of the day a woman suddenly appeared in the mill, disfigured by the sort of extreme misery affected by defendants in court. She was only semi-clothed, by a pitiful piece of patchwork. Her feet were bare and uncovered. She was yellow like boxwood and foully emaciated. Her unkempt hair was partially grey and caked in the ashes that had been scattered over it. It hung down and covered most of her face. In this state as she was, she reassuringly put her hand on the miller, as if she wished to share something with him in secret. She drew him aside to his room and, with the door put to, stayed there for an awfully long time. But when the workers had processed all the grain that they had to hand, and a further supply inevitably had to be sought, the boys came to the room and called on their master and asked for new supplies for their work. They shouted out repeatedly and frequently, but no master responded to them. They began to beat more vigorously on the door. It had been carefully bolted, and so they began to suspect that something rather serious and rather bad was afoot. With a stout shove they pushed out or broke the hinge and at last opened a way in for themselves. There was no sign of the woman, but their master was there to be seen hanging by a noose from a beam and already dead.
>
> Apuleius *Metamorphoses* 9.30

If the ghost had the physical solidity to take the miller by the hand, how did she then have the intangibility required to escape (invisibly) from the locked room? And it remains intriguingly unresolved whether she used her physical solidity to put the miller into the noose, i.e., by brute force, or merely her capacity as an intangible ghost to terrorise him into it. Similarly, in Phlegon of Tralles' (*c*. AD 140) wonderful tragic love story of the ghost of Philinnion, the ghost is able to escape the confines of its sealed vault, inevitably in the form of an intangible spirit, but then seemingly to recover its bodily physicality, first to sleep with her parents' new lodger Machates (in her childhood bedroom, we presume), and then, upon her second death, to leave a solid corpse behind beyond the confines of the vault (the corpse in the tomb subsequently being found to have disappeared).[75]

The battle of the house was to remain a key motif of the *strix* still for Gervase of Tilbury, in writing his *Otia imperiala* of AD 1209–14. Like John Damascene, he too seems to imagine that soul-flight was the key means of penetration. He tells us that his *striges* take on (as it is claimed) aerial bodies and that they pass by night over entire realms with the swiftest of flight, and then, portentously, that 'They enter houses ... '.[76]

The motif of the imperceptible penetration of the house aligns truly with another motif to which we shall turn shortly, that of the imperceptible penetration of the child's body, to work mischief within it.

2.7 Motif G: (Whole) Body-Snatching

The damage that *striges* do to babies is conceptualised in a series of partly overlapping and partly contrasting ways, as we shall investigate under the heads of this and the following three motifs: (a) they can snatch whole bodies; (b) they can steal (from without) innards and other body-parts; (c) they can extract a body's blood or moisture; and (d) they can damage the body within by (initially) imperceptible means. Here we consider the first of these.

In addition to making the claim that the *striges* had stolen the little boy's innards, Petronius' Trimalchio makes the incompatible claim that they had stolen the boy's body as a whole, replacing it with a straw doll. It is important here to bear the context of the narrative in mind. Petronius is actively projecting Trimalchio as telling a tall tale and as, in effect, carelessly making it up as he goes along, but nonetheless depending on well-established themes and motifs the while. We can be sure, accordingly, that innards-extraction and whole-body-snatching are long-hallowed paradigmatic alternates in the folktale Trimalchio is attempting to perform.

In his *Otia imperialia* of AD 1209–14, Gervase of Tilbury has much to say of *striges* that recalls the material in our three principal texts. In fact, he deploys an evolved version of the term, *stria*, which, as we have noted, he regards as a French word. The bulk of his discussion, to which we have already referred and to which we will return more than once, focuses on a variety of whole-body theft:

---

[75] Phlegon of Tralles *Mirabilia* 1; cf. Hansen 1996 *ad loc.*
[76] Gervase of Tilbury *Otia imperiala* 3.86 (pp. 39–40 Liebrecht), quoted more fully in the next section.

85. On the subject of the amazing things in this world, there is the question of *lamiae* and *draci*. Of these two classes, *lamiae* are said to be women who penetrate houses by night to disport themselves in them briefly. They open storage jars, go through baskets, pots and bowls, drag children from their cradles, kindle lamps and sometimes attack people as they sleep . . ..

86. Medical specialists affirm that *lamiae*, which are commonly termed *mascae* or, in French, *striae*, are night-time fantasies. These result from the thickening of the humours, which has an effect upon the soul as people sleep and induces the impression of tangibility. On the basis of the literary tradition, Augustine suggests that *lamiae* are demons produced from the souls of the wicked and now taking on aerial bodies.[77] They derive their name *lamiae*, or better *laniae*, from the verb *laniare* ['lacerate'], because they lacerate babies.[78] *Larvae*, by contrast, are, as it were, the fantastical visitations of *Lares*, which take on the forms and appearances of people. They are not people, but illusions taking on the shape of people by some secret divine leave. For demons can do nothing without divine leave, whether it pertains to the human body or the human mind or soul. But to make a concession to folklore, let us posit that it is the miserable fate of certain women and men to pass by night over entire realms with the swiftest of flight. They enter houses, attack people in their sleep and inflict tangible dreams upon them. By this means they make them cry out. But they also, as it would appear, eat, kindle lamps, pull people's bones apart, sometimes also fixing them back together again in a chaotic arrangement, drink human blood and transfer little children from one place to another. Imbert, the archbishop of Arles is a man of nobility, an outstanding Christian in every way, a leader of deep and proven faith and a quite pure life, and a relative of mine. He told me about something that happened to him whilst he was still taking milk. His mother was an outstanding Christian and his parents guarded him with great care. One night, in the darkness of midnight, when he was lying, swaddled, in his cradle before his parents' bed, he was heard crying. His mother, roused by the disturbance, laid her hands on the cradle, but she found in it no baby to take up. She reflected on the matter without speaking, fearing to speak but at the same time unable to endure the protracted silence. She lit a candle and searched for the baby here, there and everywhere, until she found him in a dirty puddle of the water that had been poured out after the evening washing of the feet. There he was, rolling about in it, without crying, still wearing his swaddling clothes and now briefly chuckling at his mother in the candlelight. What then? She showed the scene to the boy's nurse[79] and her husband. No one imagined that this was the work of anything other than nocturnal phantasms. For many have found that where phantasms of this sort are accustomed to disport

---

[77] Gervase seems to have in mind Augustine *City of God* 9.11, where, however, *larvae* are mentioned but *lamiae* are not; cf. Banks and Binns 2002: 727–3.

[78] This particular claim is derived from Isidore of Seville *Etymologies* 8.11.102.

[79] *nutrici*: Banks and Binns 2002 translate 'her [i.e., the mother's] nurse', presumably an elderly family retainer. But context rather demands that the interested party here should be the child's own wet-nurse, whose presence has been prepared for in the detail that he was still taking milk.

themselves, babies are discovered the next morning out of their houses and cradles and in the streets, even though the doors have been closed.
Gervase of Tilbury *Otia imperiala* 3.85–6 (pp. 39–40 Liebrecht)[80]

Gervase's protracted story here seems to combine the activities of a traditional *strix* with the less harmful ones of something more like a playful poltergeist or boggart.

2.8 Motif H: The Extraction of Innards and Body-Parts

All three of our principal sources have their *striges* extracting innards or vital organs from the children they attack. Ovid has his bird-like *striges* 'tear[ing] apart the innards of suckling babies with their beaks'. John Damascene tells that 'others say that they devour their [i.e., children's] liver'. After the *striges*' attack, the body of the baby in Petronius' story 'had no heart or guts, nothing'. Petronius refers to *striges* briefly again in another part of the *Satyricon* (and indeed on this occasion he does actually designate them *striges* as opposed to *strigae*). The context of the reference is somewhat obscure, not least because the text is damaged, but it seems that the old woman Proselenos is mocking Encolpius for his impotence with a rhetorical question: 'What *striges* have devoured your nerves [*nervos*]?', the term *nervi* also signifying, *sensu obscaeno*, 'penis'.[81] In the non-obscene sense at any rate, the question again has the *striges* devouring internal body parts. Other passing references to *striges* also salute this motif. Back in Plautus' 191 BC comedy *Pseudolus* the cook Ballio complains about his cheaper, more contemptible rivals in the trade:

> When those people cook dinners and season them, they don't season them with seasoning, but with *striges*, which are going to devour the intestines of the diners whilst they yet live. This is just the reason that people here live lives of such a short span, because they pile these sorts of herbs into their bellies – terrible things even to speak of, let alone eat.   Plautus *Pseudolus* 819–23[82]

---

[80] Cf. Banks and Binns 2002: 717–24 (notes) and Cherubini 2009b: 92, 2010a: 42–3, 2010b: 69–70. For the more immediate context of Gervase's beliefs in such phenomena, see Green 2016. Gervase's rough contemporary Walter Map wrote his *De nugis curialium* ('Courtiers' trifles') for the English court *c.* AD 1181–2. In this he tells the tale of a knight, three of whose baby sons are discovered in turn with their throats cut by night. His fourth son, however, is watched overnight by a wise pilgrim, who finds a matron leaning over the cradle to cut the child's throat. He catches hold of her until the family assembles. The malefactor is recognised as a local woman of good character, but the pilgrim insists that she is really a demon masquerading as her, out of envy, and has the real woman summoned to prove the point. When released, the demon flies away out of the window (*per fenestram auolauit*), weeping and wailing (2.14; for the text see James et al. 1983, with pp. li–lv for the date).

[81] Petronius *Satyricon* 134; cf. Friedlaender 1906: 318–22, Cherubini 2010b: 66, Schmeling 2011: 581.

[82] See Scobie 1978: 98 for the interpretation of the text; cf. also Oliphant 1913: 135–6, Cherubini 2009b: 66.

Seneca describes with some wit the ingredients his Medea blends to manufacture the napalm-like fiery substance with which she will imbue the wedding
dress of her love-rival Glauce-Creusa: 'She crops death-bringing herbs,
expresses venom from serpents and mixes evil birds in with them, the heart of
the mournful eagle-owl [*bubo*] and the innards cut from a harsh-sounding *strix*
whilst it yet lives.' Accordingly, the *strix* is to be subject to the very process –
the extraction of internal organs whilst it still lives – to which, in its woman-
reflex at any rate, it characteristically subjects its own victims.[83]

2.9 Motif I: The Extraction of Moisture

The notion that *striges* could damage a body rather by extracting moisture from
it is clearly expressed in both Ovid and John Damascene. Ovid's *striges* are said,
in general terms, to possess 'throats … engorged with the blood they have
drunk', whilst those that more specifically attack Proca are said to have 'sucked
out his infant breast with eager tongues'. John Damascene notes that 'Others say
that they devour their liver and all their moisture', the word for 'moisture' here
being the rather unusual *oikonomia*.[84] There is nothing explicit about moisture
extraction in our third key text, that of Petronius, but the witches' stuffing of the
shell of the corpse they leave behind (if that is indeed what they do) with straw
gives pause for thought, straw being a paradigmatically dry, indeed dried out,
substance.[85] Later on, Gervase of Tilbury's *lamias*, whom he identifies with
striges, are said, as we have seen, to 'drink human blood'.[86]

Propertius (*c.* 16 BC) gives us an interesting take on the motif. He tells us that
his nemesis, the bawd-witch Acanthis, 'consulted the *striges* about my blood
and gathered horse-madness [*hippomanes*], the seed of the pregnant mare, to
use against me'. Presumably this means that she asked the *striges* to syphon off
some of his blood for her so that she could use it, in the role of his 'stuff', in
a *pars pro toto* love spell against him – it is in a love spell, at any rate, that
hippomanes belongs.[87]

---

[83] Seneca *Medea* 731–4. Seneca's inclusion of *strix* body-parts in a magic potion is more pointed
than Horace's had been: the gruesome love potion that his Canidia manufactures together with
her coven at *Epodes* 5.15–24 incorporates merely 'a feather of the nocturnal *strix*' (cf. Section
3.1).
[84] For the significance of the term here, see *PG* 94, 1599–1604, *ad loc.*
[85] Indeed McDonough 1997: 320, building indirectly on Schuster 1930: 177, suggests that
Trimalchio is not speaking literally of a straw doll but of a body completely deprived of its
moisture and so resembling a straw doll. He compares *Macbeth*'s witches (I.iii.18): 'I'll drain
him dry as hay.'
[86] Gervase of Tilbury *Otia imperiala* 3.86 (pp. 39–40 Liebrecht).
[87] Propertius 4.5.17–18. For discussion see Hutchinson 2006 *ad loc.* (136–42) and Heyworth 2007
ad loc. (453–4), albeit both rather missing the point. For *hippomanes* see Tupet 1976: 79–81,
1986: 2653–7, Ogden 2009: 242–3, Cherubini 2010a: 114–17.

As female humanoids, with affinities to birds and a propensity for moisture-extraction, the *striges* might be thought to resemble the Sirens as much as they do the Harpies. The name of these mythological bird-women salutes a Greek verb (*seireō*) meaning 'to drain dry'. And, like the *striges*, the Sirens produced a notorious noise – beautiful at first, though ultimately terrible.[88]

The graphic notion that a *strix* should – on occasion at least – be possessed of bird-like, flesh-rending talons, is particularly well suited to the notion that they should steal individual body-parts or drain bodies of their blood – perhaps more closely suited to this than to the notion that they should steal whole bodies. But it is poorly adapted to other conceptualisations of the *strix*'s activities, those by which they are somehow able to destroy the child's body (initially) imperceptibly from without. It is to these that we now turn.

2.10 Motif J: Imperceptibility and the Battle of the Body

The content of the *Pseudolus* passage quoted above (Section 2.8, Motif H) could also be classified under another heading: the destruction of the body from within by surreptitious or invisible means.[89] A strong parallel obtained between the notion that a *strix* could penetrate a home by surreptitious means and the notion that she could penetrate the body of her baby-victim by surreptitious means.[90]

Other texts offer disturbing accounts of some of these surreptitious means. The second-century AD Quintus Serenus Sammonicus, tutor to the emperors Geta and Caracalla, composed a didactic hexameter poem on medicine in which he refers in passing to another second-century BC playwright, Titinius, in a brief chapter entitled 'for babies troubled by their teeth or a *strix*'.

'Nature brought man forth naked at the beginning of the world.'[91] Then she tortures him as she arms him with snowy teeth. Horse teeth, the first to fall from the mouth of the growing foal, should be tied to the child's gentle neck. Alternatively, rub the child's tender gums with the brains of a pig or a hare or the snowy milk of shaggy goats. Furthermore, if ever a black *strix* attacks

---

[88] Cf. Scobie 1978: 76. Principal sources for the Sirens include: Homer *Odyssey* 12.39–55, 165–200; Apollonius *Argonautica* 4.892–921; Apollodorus *Bibliotheca* 1.135, *Epitome* 7.18–19; Hyginus *Fabulae* 14, 125, 141; *Suda* s.v. Σειρῆνας. In general on the Sirens see Mancini 2005; for their iconography see *LIMC* s.v. *Seirenes*, with Hofstetter 1997.

[89] McDonough 1997: 318–19: 'because witches were thought to operate in a secret and backwards manner, their attacks were believed to come not from without but from within'.

[90] McDonough 1997: 331–3 draws the parallel between the penetration of the house and the penetration of the body; so too Spaeth 2010: 245–58 (but her adduction of Roman anxieties about sexual penetration seems unwarranted).

[91] Given that this line fits awkwardly with what follows – 'when mankind was first created' has to serve, in effect, for 'when a child is first born' – I take it to be a quotation from a lost source; the line of Lucretius (5.225) adduced by Brodersen 2016: 153 is not close enough.

boys, 'milking' her fetid 'dugs into their lips',[92] as they push them forth to
suck, the advice of Titinius, the composer of the celebrated toga-comedies of
yesteryear, is that they should have garlic tied to them.
Quintus Serenus Sammonicus *Liber medicinalis* 58 ll. 1029–38,[93]
incorporating Titinius F *ex incertis fabulis* xxii Ribbeck[94]

It is not clear how strong a break there is at 'Furthermore': i.e., does the
following *strix* material also refer specifically to teething, or does it refer to
a malady of another sort? In the former case, one could well understand that the
strix's evil milk causes pain directly at its point of application, just as goat's milk
(etc.) brings relief at that same point of application. In the latter case, Serenus'
reasons for bringing the treatments of the two different maladies together would
be, first, that they share a similar mode of remedy, an amulet hung around the
baby's neck, and, second, the thematic connection of milk – of some sort – going
into the baby's mouth. Given the lack of any further context for an association of
striges with teething, I am inclined to the second alternative here, but either way
the principal point in hand remains the same: an explanation is offered as to how
striges are able secretly to corrupt internal body-parts (albeit in the case of milk
teeth, only just 'internal' ones, and presumably to no great lasting effect).

The garlic plant-amulet tied around the baby offered a means to protect the
child even against *striges* that had successfully penetrated the house. Indeed, it
aligns nicely with the plant defences Ovid was subsequently to prescribe for the
protection of the outer shell of the house. It also aligns with the vast array of
more permanent amulets surviving from the late antique and Byzantine worlds,
these in the form of gemstone intaglios and metal lamellae, designed to protect
children from the depredations of child-killing demons.[95] But it was probably
possible to protect a child from an entering *strix* simply by keeping it under
constant surveillance: Ovid's note to the effect that the *striges* 'seek out children
without a nurse' suggests that, whatever their powers, surreptitious and others,
they will not normally attack a baby that is directly watched.[96]

There are further references to this phenomenon. As we have seen, it is
referred to by the sceptical Pliny, who died in AD 79 ('the claim made of *striges*,
that they milk their dugs into the lips of babies').[97] A more informative reference to it is made by Isidore of Seville in his early-seventh-century AD

---

[92] A reminiscence of Virgil *Aeneid* 11.572; cf. Brodersen 2016: 153.
[93] Text at Vollmer 1916: 49 and Brodersen 2016: 152–3 (with German trans.); cf. Phillips 2002.
[94] Text at Ribbeck 1873: 159; cf. Oliphant 1913: 136, McDonough 1997: 319, Cherubini 2010a:
    21–5, 2010b: 70–1.
[95] Discussed in detail by Björklund 2017a, 2017b, 2017c.
[96] However, the *strix*-like witch of the Walter Map tale noted in Section 2.7 goes to work undeterred
    by a vigilant watcher, though she is nonetheless thwarted by him.
[97] Pliny *Natural History* 11.232.

Etymologies: 'This bird [sc. *strix*] is commonly called *amma* from the fact that it loves [*amando*] little children, whence it is even said to offer them milk when they are born.'[98] Now, *amma* is in fact the Greek word for 'foster-mother' or 'wet-nurse'.[99] It is intriguing indeed that the *striges* should be so conceptualised as they force their destructive milk into babies. Perhaps the term was deployed in an ironic fashion, the *striges* being the worst possible of all wet-nurses – anti-nurses, even. There may be a hint of them being so conceptualised too in the Ovid passage. When he speaks of children being vulnerable to the *striges* when unguarded, he expresses the notion in a more particular way: they are vulnerable when they have no nurse present. It is perhaps implied that in the absence of the true nurse, the *strix* will take over the role, with all that that entails. Or it could be that the *striges* were addressed as *amma* for euphemistic or even propitiatory reasons: 'If we address the *strix* nicely as "foster-mother", perhaps she won't harm our baby.' We should not press Isidore's text any further. It would be interesting indeed if the terrible *striges* could be imagined – tragically? – to love the children they destroy (as it might sometimes have been believed that *lamiae* fell in love with the young men they were in train to devour).[100] However, one suspects that an understandable (though of course wholly erroneous) folk etymology linking the term *amma* in its own right and in its normal usage with the verb *amando* (*amare*) has here been imported to explain, quite inappropriately, an anomalous use of the word. Ovid perhaps constructs another ironic inversion of the true maternal role for the *striges* when he speaks of them 'sucking out the breasts' (*pectora exsorbent*) of their child-victims.[101] It is the role of the true mother, rather, to have her own breast sucked out by her baby.

Other methods of *strix* attack can also be seen as achievable surreptitiously and without leaving any immediate, external indication behind them. So it is with John Damascene's claim that *striges* can smother babies. And so it is, presumably, with the attacks that are said to drain a child of its blood or its moisture (Motif I). But the latter phenomenon may bring us back, on occasion, to suckling again. It may be that, just as the *strix* is the anti-mother or anti-nurse, so their 'feeding' of the baby works in reverse. Perhaps, whereas a normal mother or nurse gives suck to supply moisture to her baby, a *strix* gives suck precisely as a means of depriving the baby of it.

The notion of the secret penetration of the body from without in order to destroy it within is also probably to be found in Petronius' *striges* turning of the Cappadocian slave's body 'black and blue, as if he'd been beaten with whips'

[98] Isidore of Seville *Etymologies* 12.7.42; see the discussions at Oliphant 1914: 50–1, Curletto 1987: 150–1, 154–5, Cherubini 2010a: 162 n.115.
[99] LSJ *s.v.* ἀμμά. [100] Philostratus *Life of Apollonius* 4.25. [101] Ovid *Fasti* 6.145.

and then in due course in their turning of his mind mad and their killing of him: again they are corrupting the interior of his body without being seen to penetrate it or touch it. The text aligns with two others in which we have the same collocation of four motifs:

a. The action of an invisible, remote or unidentifiable power.
b. A slave victim.
c. The infliction of madness.
d. The infliction of the effects of a beating, especially a whipping.

Firstly, in Plautus' (*c.* 200 BC) comedy *Amphitruo* another slave, Sosia, has been beaten up by his own doppelganger – the god Mercury masquerading as him – and tries to explain the improbable event to his master:

AMPHITRUO:	Are you quite sane?
SOSIA:	I'm just as you see me to be.
AMPHITRUO:	Since he went away from me, this man has been touched somehow by an evil hand [*mala . . . manu*].
SOSIA:	I surely have! For I've been terribly bruised by fists!
AMPHITRUO:	Who beat you?
SOSIA:	I, who have now come home, beat myself up!

Plautus *Amphitruo* 604–7

The bracketed phrase in Trimalchio's tale – '(this was obviously because an evil hand [*mala manus*] had touched him)' – is sometimes thought to be an interpolation, an explanation mistakenly incorporated into the text from an ancient commentator's marginal note.[102] If so, the alignment with the Plautine passage confirms the commentator's acuity. Although the power that beat Sosia up was indeed visible and inflicted the beating by direct contact in the normal, physical, external fashion, there is a sense in which it becomes evanescent in Sosia's mind, given that he believes that he is himself responsible for the infliction of the beating.

Secondly, we find a similar phenomenon also in one of the tales of Lucian's (*c.* AD 170s) *Philopseudes*, where Eucrates' mysterious and powerful statue of Pellichus metes out a punishment:

Quite a few obols had been laid before his feet . . . and some other silver coins and silver leaves had been stuck to his thigh with wax, votive gifts or payments for healing from all the people he had delivered from the grip of fever. We had an accursed Libyan slave who looked after the horses. He

---

[102] E.g., by Smith 1975 *ad loc.*; Schmeling 2011 *ad loc.* appears to be happy that the phrase belongs in the original Petronian text; cf., further, Cherubini 2009a, esp. 144 n.5, 2010a: 46, 170–1 n.218.

made an attempt to steal them all during the night and steal them he did after watching for the statue to get down from his pedestal. As soon as, upon his return, Pellichus realized that he had been robbed, see how he punished the Libyan and revealed his crime. The poor man spent the entire night running round the courtyard in a circle without being able to find his way out, just as if he had been thrown into a labyrinth, until day came and he was caught with his loot. He got a good beating upon capture there and then, but he did not live very long afterwards, dying in as miserable a fashion as he deserved. As he said, he was being whipped every night, so that weals could be seen on his body on the following day.

Lucian *Philopseudes* 20[103]

Once again, we have the same quartet of motifs combined. Let us merely note that, as for motif (a), the statue, although it is capable of movement, as we learn from Lucian's foregoing introduction of it, is evidently acting remotely in this case; and as for (d), the whipping effect matches the Petronius narrative precisely. We may compare too, in a more restricted way, an episode in the originally early-third-century AD *Alexander Romance*. When Alexander's soldiers attempt to collect incense-like sap from some mysterious trees, somewhere on the far side of the Median desert, they are whipped by an 'unseen demon'. Whilst they can hear the sound of the whipping, they cannot see who is inflicting it. An invisible voice commands them to cease their activities, and Alexander accedes.[104]

This model of destruction invites comparison with another ancient (and indeed wider) phenomenon, that of the 'evil eye' (termed *fascinatio* in Latin). The evil eye was an envious look that could – even against the intentions of its deliverer – blight anything young, vigorous and developing, and so cause it to fail or waste away – human babies *in primis*, but also young animals and crops. Virgil's shepherd Menalcas accordingly complains, 'Yet as for these [sheep] . . . they scarcely stick to their bones. Some eye or other is evil-eye-ing [*oculus . . . fascinat*] my tender lambs.' The evil eye was, in short, destructive of fertility and accordingly it was combatted with amulets representing the ultimate token of fertility, the phallus. Anyone could be responsible for delivering an evil eye, but it did have a particular association with certain women, women who, like Ovid's Dipsas (for whom see Section 3.2), were possessed of double pupils. Might it also have been associated with the massive, staring eyes of owls?[105]

---

[103] The translation is taken over from Ogden 2007: 54, with exegesis of the episode at 137–60, esp. 146–8.

[104] *Alexander Romance* (Arm.) §209 Wolohojian.

[105] Virgil *Eclogues* 3.102–3; Horace *Epistles* 1.14.37–8 (*obliquo oculo*); Ovid *Amores* 1.8.15–16 (quoted above), Pliny *Natural History* 7.16–8, 28.39; Plutarch *Moralia* 680c–683b (*Table Talk* problem 7). For the evil eye in the ancient world see now Elliott 2015–17 (a four-volume study); for its manifestation in Latin poetry, Tupet 1976: 178–81, 1986: 2606–10; for its association

We should probably classify here too an interesting series of medieval Latin texts, some of which are more explicit than others about the action they are attributing to *striges*. On the clearer side is a law stipulated in the Lombardian *Edict of Rothari* of AD 643:

> No one should take it upon himself to kill another person's serving-woman or maid on the basis that she is a *striga*, also called a *masca*,[106] because such a thing should in no way be believed by Christian minds, nor does a woman have the ability to devour a person alive from the inside.
>
> *Edict of Rothari* no. 376, *MGH* Leges iv, p. 87

'Devouring a person alive from the inside' (*hominem vivum instrinsecus . . . commedere*) is suggestive of the model we have been investigating under this motif, that of the invisible, surreptitious destruction of the body from within. It is important to note the official position that such a thing is impossible, that the belief in its possibility is itself un-Christian, and that false belief in the action of *strix* is a more pressing social ill than the supposed action itself. An Alamannic law of the early seventh century AD seems to adopt a similar position:

> If a woman has called another a *stria* or a herbal witch [*erbaria*] . . . she is to pay a fine of 12 *solidi*.
>
> *Leges Alamannorum*, F2.xiii.1, *MGH* Leges nat. Germ. v.1, p. 24

Again the making of the false allegation that a woman is a *strix* is seemingly more of a threat than the supposed activities of *striges*.

Comparison of these laws in turn with the earlier *Salic Law* of King Clovis (*c.* AD 507–11) is instructive:

> If a person has called another a *hereburgius*, which is to say a *strioportius* [i.e., a (male) 'stria's porter'?], or one who is said to carry a cauldron to where the *striae* make their meal, and has not been able to substantiate the allegation, he is to be adjudged liable to pay a fine of 2,500 *denarii*, equivalent to 62½ *solidi*. If a person has called a freeborn woman a *stria* or a prostitute and has not been able to substantiate the allegation, he is to be adjudged liable to pay a fine of 7,500 *denarii*, equivalent to 187½ *solidi*. If a *stria* has eaten a person and has been convicted of it, she is to be adjudged liable to pay a fine of 8,000 denarii, equivalent to 200 solidi . . ..
>
> *Pactus legis Salicae* 63–4, *MGH* Leges nat. Germ. iv.1 p. 231[107]

---

with the *strix* in particular, Cherubini 2010a: 131–51; for its association with child-killing demons more generally, Björklund 2017a: 9–10.

[106] The meaning at this point of the term *masca*, which appears here first and is the ultimate source of the English word 'mask', can only be conjectured from context. Speculative discussion at Cherubini 2010a: 41–2, 125–30, 2010b: 68.

[107] Cf. Drew 1991 for an English translation of the *Salic Law*.

Already this law too is seemingly more concerned with the disruptive nature of false allegations of being a *strix* or, in the case of men, of taking on the role of *strix's* porter. The implicit notion that allegations of being a *strix* are more problematic when made against freeborn women than slave (or formerly slave) women intrigues, as does the fact that the same distinction is not applied in the case of their male assistants. However, unlike the *Edict*, this law does still accept that *striges* exist. Does it already impute to them a surreptitious mode of action, as in the *Edict*? Admittedly, the notion of their common feast and its cauldrons may seem to raise the possibility that the witches are devouring chunks of flesh (if not entire babies) and to speak for the open butchery of the baby victims as opposed to any surreptitious intrusion into their bodies. But this impression may be misleading: it may after all be that the feast is comprised of the softer inner organs surreptitiously removed (cf. the case of Apuleius' Socrates: Section 3.5). And here the punishment ascribed gives pause for thought: a fine, albeit a large one, seems to be an inadequate exaction for the killing and cannibalism of a baby, or indeed the mutilation of it. The relative lightness of it is perhaps more suggestive of a scenario in which a baby's failure to thrive is precariously attributed to the unseen and unprovable action of a local woman. So perhaps one can already sense here an underlying scepticism about the phenomenon that would mature into the position adopted by the *Edict of Rothari*.

This scepticism developed further in an AD 789 law Charlemagne made for the Saxons:

> If anyone is deceived by the Devil and comes to imagine, in the fashion of the pagans, that a man or a woman is a *striga* and is eating people, and for that reason burns the woman herself or gives someone her flesh to eat or eats her himself, he is to be subject to capital punishment.
>
> *Capitularia regum Francorum, Capitulatio de partibus Saxonicae* §6, MGH Leges ii.1, pp. 68–9[108]

Here the problem addressed is not the activities of *striges*, the very existence of whom is seemingly (albeit not explicitly) rejected, but the activities of those who mistakenly believe in them and accordingly take the law into their own hands. We shall have more to say about these last two interesting texts below (Section 2.13, Motif M).

Gervase of Tilbury also probably works with the surreptitious model of the *strix*'s attack on the baby's body in his *Otia imperialia* of AD 1209–14 (as quoted above, Section 2.7). The fact that he identifies *striges* with *mascae* again suggests that he is working in the same tradition as the *Edict of Rothari*. He

---

[108] Cf. Cherubini 2010a: 42, 2010b: 68, 75 (mistranslating?) and Hutton 2017: 70–1.

also identifies them with *lamiae*, before going on to speak of the latter as occupying aerial bodies (*corpora aerea*) and as lacerating babies (he borrows a folk etymology from Isidore of Seville to explain the term *lamia* as deriving from *laniare*, 'lacerate'). The fact that they are described as aerial suggests that an invisible or remote form of attack is envisaged. For Gervase *striges* can also be responsible for two further forms of externally imperceptible internal bodily attack. Firstly, the strange claim that *striges* can 'pull people's bones apart, sometimes also fixing them back together again in a chaotic arrangement' is suggestive of some sort of internal interference falling short of the instantaneous infliction of death, though precisely what is envisaged remains unclear. Secondly, they effectively penetrate the body and interfere with it internally by inflicting nightmares: they 'fly by night at great speed, enter houses, attack people in their sleep, *inflict nightmares in such a way as to make people cry out ...* '.[109] Once again, the great speed attributed to their flight here may be suggestive of an invisible soul-flight.

We noted above the parallelism between a *strix*'s penetration of the house and her penetration of the body. The parallelism presses itself upon us again here too. Just as the *striges* of Petronius and John Damascene can penetrate a house *imperceptibly*, either by virtue of magical invisibility or by virtue of soul-flying, so they can *imperceptibly* – initially, at any rate – penetrate a child's body, interfering with it from within.

2.11 Motif K: The Imposition of a Time-Limit on Life

'Others say that they devour their liver and all their moisture and impose a time-limit on their lives', observes John Damascene. In the light of this interesting claim the passage of Plautus' *Pseudolus* quoted above acquires a more pointed meaning: the *striges* that devour people's intestines whilst they yet live cause people to have lives of a short span. In other words, the lethal effects of an attack can be deferred: it need not kill immediately, but can schedule the victim for death at a later stage.[110] The significance of this motif will come across more vividly when we come to consider its impact upon one of the non-*strix* texts in the following section, namely Apuleius' account of the death of Socrates (Section 3.5).

2.12 Motif L: Fighting Back against the *Strix*

The motif-set we are reconstructing, partly on the basis of the brief narratives of Ovid and Petronius, builds to a larger ideal story. But what endings are possible

[109] Gervase of Tilbury *Otia imperiala* 3.85–6 (pp. 39–40 Liebrecht).
[110] Plautus *Pseudolus* 819–23.

for this story? Must it end either, like Ovid's, with the thwarting of the *strix* in the course of her attack, with plant-amulets, or like Petronius', with the victory of the *strix*? Could the ideal narrative progress to a further, and quite satisfactory, stage, with a victory over the *strix* after an initially successful attack on her part? Perhaps it could, the key to this lying in Charlemagne's AD 789 Saxon law, as quoted above (Section 2.10).[111] This seemingly reports a pagan scenario in accordance with which a person who believes a woman to be a *strix* and to be eating people will burn her and give her flesh to someone else to eat, or eat it himself. What is envisaged here? One might think first of some sort of eye-for-an-eye variety of revenge. But what are we to make of the curious emphasis on the giving of her flesh to someone else to eat, this prospect being stipulated before that of the eating of it oneself? This is the clue. Surely, what is envisaged is a situation in which a parent cooks the flesh of a *strix* and feeds it back to his failing baby, so that the baby may recover the organs, or the moisture, that the *strix* has herself devoured from it. Such a notion may be as old as that of the Roman *strix* itself. Let us recall that Plautus (as quoted above, Section 2.8, Motif H) already jokes about bad cooks cooking *striges* and feeding them to people to eat, whereupon, somehow still alive, they continue to devour their eaters' insides. The joke gains greater purchase if the broader notion that one might cook and eat a (dead) *strix* was already established.[112]

The notion that one could recover and restore to working order one's extracted organs by eating the flesh of the one that had digested them will strike moderns as absurd. But such a notion could perhaps pass in the logic of folktale. A partial justification for it is to be found in a fascinating modern Greek folktale published by Polites in 1871. A man is staying overnight as a guest in his friend's house. From his bed he hears his friend's wife and her mother planning to eat either him or the friend, depending upon whichever is the fatter. They lift one of the feet of each man by turn to see which is heavier, but the guest lifts his foot with them to make them think it is the lighter one. So the friend is chosen as the victim: the women rip out his liver and innards and throw them in the ashes to cook. Realising they are short of wine for their meal, they fly (NB) out to the wine shop. In the meantime, the guest scoops his friend's innards up into his bag and replaces them with some animal dung. The witches return for their meal, find it disappointing but suspect nothing. The next morning the two men leave the house. The friend shows no sign of a wound, but is very pale. He complains that he is exceedingly hungry, whereupon the friend gives him his own innards to eat from his bag; having them back inside him, he is fully restored. The guest

---

[111] *Capitularia regum Francorum, Capitulatio de partibus Saxonicae* §6, *MGH* Leges ii.1, pp. 68–9.

[112] Plautus *Pseudolus* 819–23.

explains to his friend what he has witnessed during the night. They return to the house and kill the witches. (The tale constitutes a striking partial analogue for Apuleius' tale of Meroe, Panthia, Socrates and Aristomenes, discussed in Section 3.5.)[113]

2.13 Motif M: The *Strix* Coven – and Cooking

Striges are often held to work in a group – perhaps we may say, to the extent that they can be identified with witches, a 'coven'.[114] Ovid's Proca is attacked by plural *striges*. Petronius' plural *striges* arguably make their attack with a co-ordinated and co-operative plan: some screech outside the house to trick the occupants into opening the door; one of them sacrifices herself to the Cappadocian's sword; another, or others, of them in the meantime slip within the house to make their depredations on the baby's body. But the most intriguing text here, albeit frustratingly allusive, is the *c.* AD 507–11 *Salic Law* of King Clovis, quoted above (Section 2.10, Motif J). This seems to construct a vignette in which the *striges* meet together, seemingly in a special place, to participate in a communal feast consisting of the cooked body-parts or possibly the whole bodies they have stolen. In this they enjoy the support of male assistants, who carry the cauldron for them – either to the special place, or at it, i.e., in the role of kitchen assistants or waiters. Do they cook the meat for them too? Do they themselves eat too? Charlemagne's Saxon law of AD 789 (also quoted above, Section 2.10, Motif J, again) is framed in such a way as to seem to allow for the possibility of males of full *strix* status, although its focus remains on the female ones, as we should expect. And in speaking of the possibility of people burning *striges* in a seemingly reciprocal context, this law also seems to assume that the *striges* cook their food before eating it. The *Salic Law* is particularly striking for giving us a unique glance of *striges* going about their business in a location other than the site of their attacks, the baby-victim's house or bedroom.[115]

---

[113] Polites 1871: 179–81; see also Lawson 1910: 182–3.

[114] Witch-covens are rare in Classical literature. We may mention the following. (a) Sophron's (v BC) mime *Women Who Claim to Drive out the Goddess* seems to have portrayed a presiding witch directing a mixed group dominated by women in the performance of a spell (FF3–4; cf. the sceptical Hordern 2004 *ad loc.*). (b) Sophocles' (v BC) Medea-focused tragedy *Root-Cutters* (*Rhizotomoi*) was evidently named for a chorus consisting of a group of (surely female) herbal witches. (c) Theocritus' Simaetha (270s BC) is assisted in her love spell by her maid, Thestylis (*Idylls* 2). (d) In poems of *c.* 30 BC Horace's Canidia is on one occasion supported by a single companion, Sagana (*Satires* 1.8), and on another by three, Sagana now joined by Veia and Folia (*Epodes* 5; cf. Section 3.1). (e) At Ovid *Fasti* 2.572–83 (*c.* AD 8) an old woman passes on the technique of tongue-binding magic to a class of girls.

[115] *Pactus legis Salicae* 63–4, *MGH* Leges nat. Germ. iv.1 p. 231. The practices implied here coincide in a striking way with those allegedly uncovered in an AD 1452 witch trial at Provins, near Paris, as reported at Kieckhefer 1998: 101: 'rather than sucking the infants' blood in their homes as they lay by their mothers, the witches brought the infants' bodies to their assemblies

2.14 Motif N: The Folktale and the Folkloric

The motif we discuss here is of a different sort, being resident not within any of the ancient narratives (or implied narratives) in question, but attached to them from without: it could be termed a 'meta-narrative' motif. This motif, by different methods, projects the narratives in question as folkloric, as, that is to say, belonging to a world of popular oral story-telling and popular wisdom.[116] As we have seen (Section 2.3, Motif C), Pliny confines the claim that *striges* milk their dugs into the lips of babies to the realm of stories (*fabulosum*).[117] And then Gervase of Tilbury (AD 1209–14) introduces his discussion of the *strix* with a striking phrase we have rendered above with 'But to make a concession to folklore.' More literally, the phrase reads, 'But to make a concession to the usages and the ears of ordinary people [*moribus ac auribus hominum*].' Gervase contrasts this tradition with the literary tradition, the 'words of authors' (*ex dictis auctorum*), that he has been discussing hitherto.[118]

Each of our three key texts projects their *strix* material into the realm of folklore by different means. John Damascene does it in the simplest fashion by attributing the claims about *striges* he discusses to 'some less well-educated people', before going further and scornfully associating them with heretics, deceivers of the faithful and would-be destroyers of the Church.

As noted, the *strix* tale Petronius gives to Trimalchio is presented as one of a pair exchanged between barely educated and gullible diners at a nouveau-riche dinner party, where it responds to a werewolf story narrated by his fellow freedman Niceros. Niceros tells how, when still a slave, he set out one night to visit his girlfriend Melissa in her pub and persuaded his master's house-guest, a soldier, to accompany him. The moon was shining brightly when they arrived amongst some roadside tombs and the soldier paused, ostensibly to pee against one of them. But Niceros noticed that the soldier was taking his clothes off. He laid them beside the road, peed a circle around them, turned into a wolf, howled and ran off into the woods. When Niceros made to pick the clothes up, he found they had been turned to stone. He continued on his journey to his girlfriend's, now in a state of terror. Upon arrival Melissa told him that a wolf had just got in amongst their flocks and wrought much havoc, but that one of their slaves had driven a spear through its neck and chased it off. He ran off home in more terror still. When he came to the tombs, the clothes were gone but the spot where they had been was covered in blood. When he finally got home he found the soldier

---

(often known as a "synagogue" or a *chète*), where they were eaten. Often it is specified that the infants were killed, buried, exhumed, roasted and then eaten ... the witches included men as well as women.' Kieckhefer collects much XV AD material of interest for our subject.
[116] Cf., generally, Scobie 1978.   [117] Pliny *Natural History* 11.232.
[118] Gervase of Tilbury *Otia imperiala* 3.86 (pp. 39–40 Liebrecht).

back in human form, lying abed with a doctor tending to the wound in his neck, and he realised that he was a werewolf.[119] We are, accordingly, given the impression that *striges* and werewolves belong together in the same extravagant and atmospheric story-world. Niceros finishes his tale with the declaration, 'Others can make up their own mind about this, but if I'm lying, may your guardian spirits exercise their wrath upon me', and by doing so contrives to underline the tale's tall status, rather than the opposite. Roman dinner parties were indeed appropriate places for tall tales. Rich Romans, including the emperor Augustus himself, even brought professional story-tellers, *aretalogi*, into them, as Suetonius recounts. We get an idea of the tallness of the stories such men might typically tell when the satirist Juvenal describes Odysseus as a 'lying *aretalogus*', this in connection with his recounting of his marvellous tales of the Cyclopes and the Laestrygonians to Alcinous over dinner.[120]

Ovid nods to the folkloric origin of his material in a more sophisticated way. His Cranae-Carna seemingly undergoes a third mutation after becoming a goddess from a woodland nymph. In the portion of the narrative quoted she is cast in the role of an (elderly?) local wise woman: we get the impression of a friendly crone, indeed of a benign elderly witch, an equal and opposite of Ovid's old-women *striges*, though admittedly nothing is explicitly said to this effect. At any rate, the notion is conveyed that the protective whitethorn belongs to the realm of folk wisdom – and if the remedy belongs here, then so, of course, must the lore that justifies its virtue.

2.15 Conclusion: The *Strix*-Paradigm

We conclude by building an ideal narrative of a *strix* attack – which we may term 'the *strix*-paradigm' – extrapolated from the material and the motifs considered in this section, and depending wholly upon texts that explicitly deploy the term *strix*:

> The *strix* is a terrible woman that attacks babies. She flies by night to make her attack, and to do so she transforms herself into a bird, screeching as she goes (hence her name) or else into a bird-like creature, or again she dispatches her soul from her body on a soul-flight. It is the shell of the house in which the baby sleeps that constitutes the initial focus of the battle between the *strix* and its protecting household (parents, nurses). The *strix* must find her way inside it by virtue of a trick. If she is soul-flying, the soul can infiltrate the house by passing through tiny cracks. Otherwise the witch can infiltrate the house in

---

[119] Petronius *Satyricon* 61–2. This tale has received rather more scholarly attention than the *strix* tale with which it is paired: see the items collected at Ogden 2021: 1–2.

[120] Suetonius *Augustus* 74; Juvenal *Satires* 15.16. For aretalogy of this sort, and more on the sorts of contexts in which the Romans expected to tell tall tales, see Ogden 2021: 208–10.

full body by rendering herself invisible, tricking the householders into opening their door and then slipping through it surreptitiously. The battle is not entirely one-sided: the householder has means to defend against the *strix* too: he can, on some occasions at least, merely keep his door shut, or otherwise protect it with arbutus, and his windows with whitethorn. Nonetheless, once the *strix* has gained access to the baby within, she can attack it in a number of ways: she can simply steal its entire body; she can rend its liver or its other inner organs from it, with her talons if in bird or semi-bird form; she can deprive it of its moisture. She can blight the child in a surreptitious way, for example by suckling it with her toxic milk, or again by spiriting away its internal organs, somehow or other, without leaving a scar. These latter techniques do not kill the child at once, but destine it for death at a later point, after a slow decline. The initially invisible and surreptitious infiltration of the body of the child mirrors that of the house itself. It may have been held that the child could recover the internal organs the *strix* had devoured if the *strix* could be captured and fed back to it in turn.

The default assumption is that the *striges* simply devour the bodies, the body-parts or the moisture of the babies they steal. No doubt they have a rejuvenating effect. But the evidence considered in the next section (esp. 3.1, 3.5; cf. 3.4) raises the possibility that they could sometimes rather retain the material to deploy it for magical purposes.

3 Roman Witches: The Impact of the *Strix*-Paradigm

We have seen how the *strix* can be identified with the witch (2.1). In this section we now turn to more general portraits of witches in Latin literature, portraits in which the term *strix* is not deployed, but which appear nonetheless to have been influenced by the *strix*-paradigm. The *strix*-paradigm appears to offer a gateway for the representation of witches as bloodthirsty, morbid, gruesome and gory in all things, and so to account for the radical difference in the general representation of witches in Latin literature from their representation in the Greek literature that preceded it and was in most respects its principal inspiration.

3.1 Horace's Canidia

In the figure of Canidia Horace offers us, across a cycle of six poems written *c.* 30 BC, the earliest extant developed portrait of a witch in Latin literature, and indeed the earliest extant developed portrait of a hag witch in the western tradition. A number of her features make appeal to the *strix*. Most strikingly, in a poem of the *Epodes*, he tells how she and her coven of fellow witches, Sagana, Veia and Folia, have kidnapped a boy in order to manufacture a love potion she can use against Varus. They bury him up to his neck inside their house – presumably in the peristyle court – and starve him to death, whilst instilling a sense of longing into his parts by laying out food before him three times a day, just beyond the reach of his mouth: 'This was so that his moisture-less marrow and dried liver could form a love-potion.' So here we have the motifs of an old-woman witch (Motif A); of child-stealing, albeit of a child rather older than a baby (Motif G); of body-part extraction, including that of the liver, albeit probably, though not necessarily, after death (Motif H); and of moisture extraction (Motif I). A nod is in fact made to the *strix* itself in the detail that Canidia burns a *strix* feather in her preparatory sacrifice.[121] In another poem of the *Epodes* it seems that Horace is accusing Canidia of extracting his own moisture: 'My youth has fled and my blushing colour has abandoned my bones to leave them wrapped in a sallow skin.' Perhaps we should associate this with Canidia's declaration that she has imposed a time-limit on his life: 'But death awaits you, a slower one than that for which you will pray. Your thankless, wretched life is to be extended to this end, so that you may continue to be available for torture' (Motif K).[122]

There are plenty of other gruesome details in the cycle to go with these. In the former of these *Epodes* poems Canidia is said to keep vipers entwined in her hair.[123] In the *Satires* we learn how, accompanied by Sagana alone this time, Canidia attempts another kind of love spell, exploiting the ghosts of a former cemetery. They dig into the earth with their long fingernails to make an offering pit. They tear a sacrificial lamb apart with their own mouths and fill the pit with its blood, before negotiating with the summoned ghosts. They are chased off mid-spell when a guardian statue of Priapus 'farts' at them, as the wood from which it is made splits. In their hasty departure they are revealed for the crones they are, for, as we have seen, Canidia leaves her false teeth behind, Sagana her wig.[124]

3.2 Ovid's Bawd-Witch Dipsas

The poems of Latin love elegy are stalked by the stock figure of the old and drunken bawd-witch, the wicked crone who controls the lover's girlfriend, presses her to extract large sums of money from him, or tries to tempt her

---

[121] Horace *Epodes* 5 (the quotation is of lines 37–8). Kieckhefer 1998: 95–6 reports on the trial for witchcraft of Filippa of Città della Pieve in Perugia, AD 1455. The activities of which she was accused resemble both those of a *strix* and those of Canidia more particularly. The Devil would transport Filippa and the witch-mistress to whom she was apprenticed wherever they wished to go. Thus transported into the house of a neighbour, the pair sucked the blood from a baby boy as he slept with his mother, inducing his death. They subsequently dug his body up again, dismembered it by boiling and made a magical powder from his bones and candles from his fat.

[122] Horace *Epodes* 17.21–2.   [123] Horace *Epodes* 5.15.

[124] Horace *Satires* 1.8. The other poems of the cycle are *Epodes* 3 and (with brief mentions only) *Satires* 2.1 and 2.8. For Canidia see Watson 2003 on *Epodes* 5 and 17, Cherubini 2010a: 100–14, 2010b: 68; cf. also Paule 2017: 67–72.

away from him into the embrace of a richer lover. Tibullus and Propertius both put examples of the type before us,[125] but it is the Dipsas, with a speaking name signifying 'Drunken', of Ovid's (c. 16 BC) *Amores* that claims our attention here:

> There is this (listen up, if you want to learn about a bawd!), there is this old woman called Dipsas . . . I suspect that she shape-shifts and flits about among the shades of the night [*nocturnas versam volitare per umbras*] and that her old woman's body is covered with feathers [*pluma corpus anile tegi*]. This is what I suspect, and this is what they say. Also, double pupils flash from her eyes, and the beams shine from twin circles . . . . This woman set herself the task of violating the chastity of my girl's bedroom [*thalamos temerare pudicos*]. It must be said, her tongue does have a destructive eloquence.
>
> Ovid *Amores* 1.8.1–2, 13–16, 19

Ovid does not give us the word *strix*, but Dipsas' assimilation to such a creature is self-evidently strong: she operates by night (Motif B) and she shape-shifts into a bird (Motif C). And we have noted the similarities between the *strix*'s work and that of the evil eye (Motif J). Given this, Ovid's claim that Dipsas violates the chastity of his girlfriend's bedroom is particularly suggestive. The old woman's attempt to suborn Ovid's girl into taking another lover is wittily assimilated to the mission of the *strix*-proper to violate the protective space of the baby's bedroom (Motif F). Starting from this *strix*-like base, Ovid broadens out to include further gory horrors in the woman's magical repertoire: she makes the stars drip with blood, she calls the long-dead out of their graves and opens up the earth (down to the underworld, presumably).[126]

3.3 The Snatching of Iucundus

At this point we insert into our series of treatments of passages from Latin literature a text of a rather different sort, an inscribed epitaph from Rome of around the early AD 20s, which also in its own way makes appeal to the imagery of the *strix*. As often in ancient epitaphs, the voice belongs to the deceased:[127]

> **Iucundus, the slave of Livia the wife of Drusus Caesar, son of Gryphus and Vitalis.** As I grew towards my fourth year I was seized and killed, when I had the potential to be sweet for my mother and father. I was snatched by a witch's hand [*saga manus*], ever cruel so long as it remains on the earth and does harm with its craft. Parents, guard your children well [*concustodite*], lest grief of this magnitude should implant itself in your breast.
>
> *CIL* vi.19747 = *ILS* 8522 = *CLE* 987

---

[125] Tibullus 1.5, esp. 39–59; Propertius 4.5, esp. 4.5.1–18, 63–78.
[126] Ovid *Amores* 1.8.11, 17–18. For general discussion of the poem see McKeown 1989: 198–212; cf. also Cherubini 2010a: 26–7, 117–19.
[127] Cf., generally, Lattimore 1942.

One would give much to know more about the context of Iucundus' dis-
appearance, but perhaps there was nothing more to say. One imagines that the
boy simply went missing one day and that his slave parents and the princess
Livia (more usually known as 'Livilla') alike merely reached out for the
folkloric explanation that had, after all, been developed precisely to account
for this sort of thing. We note how these brief words, not least in their final
appeal, indirectly construct the scenario of a child's parents or guardians
protecting it within the house as the *strix* comes hunting for it from without.
The guarding envisaged here may be a very direct one: as we noted above, it
may be that *striges* would not attack a child that was physically attended or
watched by a guardian (Motif J).

Two brief observations on the phrase 'witch's hand', *saga manus*. First,
strictly speaking, this is an over-translation, the Latin stipulating only 'by
a wise hand'; in such a context 'wise' is inevitably used in the specialised
sense of 'knowing magic', but it might be thought that it does not itself entail
that the culprit is female as such. However, the feminine adjective qualifying the
word for 'hand' and signifying 'wise' here, *saga*, was often used substantively –
as a noun – to mean a 'wise woman', i.e., a 'magic-knowing woman', 'a witch'
(cf. Horace's Sagana). It is difficult to believe, accordingly, that the adjectival
saga of the inscription is not imbued with the connotations of its substantive
counterpart, and one imagines that it would indeed have triggered an image of
a witch in the minds of the first Romans that read it. Secondly, why the focus on
the hand anyway? The phrase *saga manus* ('wise-(woman)-hand') resembles
a calque on the *mala manus* ('evil hand'), that tool of surreptitious destruction
we have seen to be particularly associated with the *striges* in the Petronian text
(whether an interpolation or not).

3.4 Lucan's Erictho

In an elaborate 400-line episode of Lucan's (AD 65) *Pharsalia*, Sextus Pompey
conceives the desire to divine the outcome of the civil war between his father,
Pompey the Great, and Julius Caesar, and he turns to the horrid Thessalian witch
Erictho for help.[128] She undertakes to perform for Sextus the surest form of
divination, necromancy. This is achieved by summoning back from the underworld the soul of a recently dead soldier and reinserting it into his mangled
body, to reanimate it. Erictho's principal affinity with the *strix* is the delight she
takes in the gory and invasive collection of body-parts for her magic, as Lucan
explains in the lengthy introduction with which he favours her:

---

[128] Lucan *Pharsalia* 413–830. For general discussion of Erictho see Gordon 1987, Korenjak 1996,
Ogden 2001: 202–5, 2008: 51–6, Cherubini 2010a: 120–4, 2010b: 68.

She buries in the tomb souls that are still living and governing their limbs, while death comes, despite itself, upon those to whom the fates still owe years of life. She turns the cortege around and brings the funeral back from the tomb. The corpses escape death. She snatches from the middle of pyres the smoking ashes of the young, together with their burning bones. She collects the very torch that the parents held, the remains of the funereal bier, fluttering about in black smoke, the clothes as they dissolve into cinders, and the ashes that smell of burnt limbs. But when the corpses are preserved in stone coffins, through the action of which their innermost moisture is drained and the bodies dry out, the corruption of the marrow drawn off, then she greedily exercises her cruelty on all the limbs. She plunges her hands into the eyes and delights to have dug out the frozen balls. She gnaws at the pale nails of the dried-out hand. She breaks with her jaws the noose and its harmful knots. She plucks at the hanging corpse and scrapes off crosses. She tears at guts beaten upon by rainstorms and bone marrow roasted in the rays of the sun. She takes the iron nail that pierces the hands, the corrupt black matter that runs over the limbs, and the congealed slime. She hangs off muscles that are resistant to her bite. And, should a body be lying on exposed ground, she takes up her position beside it before the wild beasts and the carrion birds arrive. She has no wish to harvest the limbs with a knife or her own hands. Rather, she waits for the wolves to bite it so that she can snatch the pieces from their unmoistened jaws. Her hands do not hesitate to slaughter, if living blood is required, of the kind that is the first to burst forth when a throat is opened, and her funereal tables demand entrails still aquiver. Babies are dragged out from a slashed-open belly, not the way nature intended, to be laid upon hot altars. Whenever she needs cruel and brazen shades, she herself manufactures the ghosts. Every human death is of some use to her. She tears the blooming cheek from the body of a young man. She cuts the lock with her left hand from the dying adolescent. Often too, at the funeral of a relation the dreadful Thessalian presses herself upon his limbs, dear to her as they are, and, while fixing kisses upon them, hacks bits off his head. With her teeth she releases the mouth, frozen shut, and, biting the end of the tongue that sticks fast in the dry throat, pours mutterings between the chill lips and sends secret and criminal orders down to the Stygian ghosts.   Lucan *Pharsalia* 6.530–69

It is noteworthy that in collecting body-parts from corpses, outer and inner ones alike (Motif H), Erictho particularly favours those from which the moisture has been drained (Motif I). She can be seen to outstrip the common-or-garden *strix* in her desire for baby-flesh, preying not merely on the new-born but actually on foetuses (Motif G).

As she proceeds to the focal reanimation, her operations on the corpse both salute and invert the standard activities of the *strix*:

Then she opened up the chest with further wounds and filled it with seething blood. She rinsed the innards of corrupt matter and unstintingly administered

moon-juice. In this was mixed whatever creature nature had produced under ill
omen.   Lucan *Pharsalia* 6.667–80

She opens up the corpse's chest not to extract its blood and its moisture, but
rather to fill it with new blood and moon-juice liquid, this imbued with
a dizzying array of magical ingredients, as Lucan goes on to describe (Motif
I again). She handles the corpse's innards, although this is not to extract them,
but rather to purify them (Motif H again).

Lucan's portrait of Erictho finally makes an acknowledgement, albeit
a passing one, of the *strix* herself (or itself) in the inarticulate, bestial howl
she emits in the course of her reanimation spell:

> Then her voice, mightier than all the herbs in the bewitching of the gods of
> Lethe, poured out, first, mutterings that were discordant and not all of which
> sounded like the products of a human tongue. The voice contained the barking
> of dogs and the howling of wolves, the complaining cries of a scared eagle-owl
> [*bubo*] and the nocturnal *strix*, the screeching and bellowing of wild animals,
> and the hissing of the snake.   Lucan *Pharsalia* 6.685–90

Like the *strix*, Erictho is a screecher (Motif E), but the noise that she makes
far exceeds their cries in its terrible sound.

3.5 The Thessalian Witches of Apuleius' *Metamorphoses*

Given the close engagement of Apuleius' (later ii AD) *Metamorphoses* or
Golden Ass with the *strix*-paradigm, it is remarkable that the word does not
appear anywhere in the novel. We shall consider three episodes from the text's
first three books, in reverse order of their appearance.

The novel's pivotal episode takes place in the third book, where the hero
Lucius accidentally turns himself into an ass, and spends the remainder of the
novel in a series of adventures as he attempts to recover his human form. What
he had been trying to do, however, was turn himself rather into an owl, having
just secretly watched the witch Pamphile, the mistress of his slave-girlfriend
Photis, achieve this very feat, as a means of flying off to meet her lover. This is
how Photis describes Pamphile's rooftop workshop:

> As night began ... my lady Pamphile ... went up onto a shingled terrace on
> the other side of the house. It is open and exposed to the winds and affords
> views in all directions, especially the east. She frequents this place secretly,
> since it is so useful for her magical crafts. First, she organized her laboratory
> of death with her usual equipment. It was full of every sort of spice, metal
> tablets with undecipherable inscriptions, and preserved pieces of shipwrecks,
> and it included an array of quite a few parts from mourned and even from
> buried corpses. Here there were noses and fingers, there nails from the

crucified, flesh still clinging to them. Elsewhere she kept the gore of the slain and mutilated skulls twisted from the jaws of wild animals.

Apuleius *Metamorphoses* 3.17

And this is the scene in which Lucius watches her transform in the workshop:

... one day Photis ran up to me quivering with excitement. She told me that her mistress, since she was having no success in consummating her love with her other techniques, was going to grow feathers and become a bird during the following night and fly down to the man she desired. Accordingly, she bade me prepare myself carefully to watch this great spectacle. Then, around the first watch of the night, she led me herself up to that upper room. We tiptoed quietly. She told me to watch what went on through some crack in the door [*perque rimam ostiorum quampiam*]. This is what I saw. First Pamphile divested herself of all her clothes. She opened a casket and took a few little boxes from it. She took the top off one of these and scooped some lotion out of it. For a while she worked it between her palms and then she smeared herself all over with it, from the ends of her toenails to the hairs on the top of her head. She had a mysterious conversation with her lamp and set her limbs fluttering. As they gently flowed, soft down sprung from them, and strong feathers grew. Her nose grew hard and became hooked, and her toenails curved round into talons. An eagle-owl [*bubo*] was made of Pamphile. With this she issued a mournful screech [*stridore*] and, testing herself, jumped up from the ground, a little higher each time. Then she pulled herself aloft and flew out of the house, using the full power of her wings.

Apuleius *Metamorphoses* 3.21[129]

We can see a number of *strix*-themes refracted in these two passages: the nocturnal setting (Motif B); the self-transformation into an owl (Motif C); the screeching (Motif E); and the collection of body-parts (Motif H). Perhaps even the crack in the door through which Lucius watches the transformation salutes the tiny chink in the protective circuit of a house through which a soul-projecting *strix* can insert herself (Motif D). We may also note that Pamphile's workshop is essentially a rooftop in itself, which is suggestive in light of Tibullus' curse against his bawd-witch: 'May ghosts ever flit about her complaining of their fates and may the *strix* call from her roof.'[130]

Apuleius seems to work hard to project Pamphile as almost a *strix*, but not quite. The variety of owl into which he has her change herself is specified to be not a *strix* but a (nonetheless screeching) *bubo*, an eagle-owl.[131] However, this

---

[129] For commentary on this episode, see Van der Paardt 1971 *ad loc.*; cf. also Frangoulidis 2008: 48–55.

[130] Tibullus 1.5.51–2.

[131] The *Onos* is an expansive summary of the lost Greek (Lucianic?) novel, *Metamorphōseōn logoi diaphoroi*, upon which Apuleius based the principal narrative skeleton of his *Metamorphoses* (Bremmer 1998: 167–71 dates the *Metamorphōseōn logoi diaphoroi* to *c.* AD 170 and Apuleius'

was an owl with which the pure-bird *strix* often found itself in company in Latin texts, and when they are brought together attention is called to the fact that the *bubo* makes a terrible noise of its own, just as the *strix* does. Ovid places the two varieties together in an evil tree ('It provides foul shade to screeching [*raucis*] *bubones*; in its branches it holds the eggs of the vulture and the *strix*').[132] Seneca's Medea combines elements from both birds in the toxic brew she prepares with which to burn Glauce-Creusa to death ('the heart of the mournful [*maesti*] *bubo* and the innards cut from a screeching [*raucae*] *strix* whilst it yet lives').[133] In the same poet's *Hercules Furens* the *bubo* and the *strix* sit beside the Cocytus in the underworld, with the former complaining (*gemit*) and the latter making the sound of a grim omen (*omenque triste resonat*).[134] The inarticulate howl with which Lucan's Erictho accompanies her reanimation spell combines the sounds of both together, as we have just seen ('the laments [*queruntur*] of the *bubo*, and those of the nocturnal *strix*').[135] A dire augury of Statius comprises 'the complaints [*gemunt*] of nocturnal *striges* and the funereal song of the *bubo*'.[136] Pliny presents the *bubo* as possessed of a (*strix*-like) complaint (*gemitus*) as opposed to a song, and as a funereal bird portentous of evil, not least when it appears in an urban context, which broadly reminds us again of Tibullus' *strix* calling from the bawd's roof.[137]

Even though the owl featured here is specified to be the *bubo* rather than the *strix*, Apuleius' narrative is precious for giving us a vivid impression of how a Roman might have visualised the process by which *strix*-women transformed themselves before proceeding to their night's work.

Our second witch-episode of interest in the *Metamorphoses* comes in a story related by one Thelyphron. He tells how as a young man on his travels through Thessaly he had looked to make some money for the road by volunteering to watch a corpse overnight before its burial, to protect it from the local witches that would attempt to cull body-parts from it for use in their love magic. He receives stern advice about how the witches operate, and about local laws:

> One must focus one's eyes continuously on the corpse, straining them and not allowing them to blink. One must never divert one's gaze, or even glance to the side, because those hateful women can skin-shift into any animal and sneak in secretly in new guise. They could easily get the better even of the eyes of the Sun, or of Justice. For they take on the forms of birds, or again of

---

version to *c*. AD 180). In the *Onos* the bird into which the parallel character, the wife of Hipparchus, transforms herself is described as a 'night crow' (*korax nykterinos*, 12). It is just possible that this obscure term could have included the *strix* in its semantic field; cf. Scobie 1978: 77–80, Cherubini 2010a: 27.

[132] Ovid *Amores* 1.12.19–20. Cf. Oliphant 1913: 138–9, 146–7, Scobie 1978: 77–80.
[133] Seneca *Medea* 732–3.   [134] Seneca *Hercules Furens* 687–8.   [135] Lucan *Pharsalia* 6.689.
[136] Statius *Thebaid* 3.511–12.   [137] Pliny *Natural History* 10.34–5; Tibullus 1.5.52.

dogs and mice, and even of flies. Then, with their awful spells, they bury the watchers in sleep. No one could begin to estimate the number of ruses these evil women devise to service their lust. But no more than four or, perhaps, six gold pieces are offered in reward for this job, as deathly as it is. And oh yes! – the thing I almost left out: if a watcher does not return the corpse in one piece the next morning, he is forced to repair any part of the corpse that has been chopped off or mutilated by having it cut from his own face.

Apuleius Metamorphoses 2.22

Despite the warning, Thelyphron takes the job on:

So I was left alone to comfort the corpse. I gave my eyes a rubbing and armed them for the night watch. I calmed my mind by singing, through twilight, evening, then bedtime, and finally the depth of the night. I was sinking under an increasing burden of fear, when suddenly a weasel crept in and stood opposite me. It directed a piercing stare toward me. I was disconcerted by the extraordinary self-confidence of this tiny animal. Eventually I said to it, 'Off with you, dirty creature, go and hide with the mice you resemble! Otherwise, you will soon feel my might. Off with you!' It turned tail and disappeared at once from the room. But all of a sudden a profound sleep suddenly plunged me to the depth of an abyss. I slept so fast that not even Apollo of Delphi himself could easily have told which of the two of us lying there was the more dead. So lifeless was I, and so much in need of a watcher in turn, that I may as well not have been there.   Apuleius *Metamorphoses* 2.25

When, finally, he wakes again in the morning, the initially panic-stricken Thelyphron is relieved to find that the corpse remains intact after all. The subsequent funeral is interrupted by the dead man's father, who brings forward an Egyptian wizard, Zatchlas, to reanimate his son's corpse in order to confirm his suspicion that he had been poisoned by his wife (another witch, we may think), and this indeed the dead man does, before proceeding:

'I will give it you, I will give you clear proof that I speak pure truth, and, moreover, I shall tell you something that no one knows or has divined.' Then he pointed me out with his finger. 'For while this shrewd watcher was attentively guarding my body, some old-women enchanters [*cantatrices*] threatened my remains. To this end they repeatedly shifted shape, but in vain, because they could not get the better of his zealous diligence. In the end they threw a mist of sleep over him and buried him in deep oblivion. Then they summoned me by my name until my slow joints and cold limbs began to strain to comply with their magical art, struggling heavily. But since this man was actually alive, and merely dead with sleep, and because he is my namesake, he rose unknowingly in response to his name and walked auto-matically like a lifeless ghost. The doors to the bedroom had been locked tight, but he suffered the butchery in my place with first his nose and then his ears being cut off through a hole. To tidy up after their trick, they moulded

Magic

some wax into the shape of his chopped-off ears, fitted them onto him in exact
fashion, and got him a nose like his own. And now the poor man stands here,
after winning not a reward for work but compensation for mutilation.'

Apuleius Metamorphoses 2.30[138]

This tale too refracts a number of *strix* themes. Firstly, the witches are old
women (Motif A). Secondly, they are faced with the special challenge of how to
enter a locked room (Motif F). Thirdly, they use animal-transformation to
overcome the problem; although the featured transformation is into a weasel,
we note that the initial advice to Thelyphron specifies birds first in the list of the
creatures into which the witches can transform themselves (Motif C). Fourthly,
they also make use of chinks in the wall – to work through, if not to pass through
in the fashion of a projected soul (Motif D). Fifthly, it is their mission to cull
body-parts (Motif H). Sixthly, they damage their victim's body surreptitiously,
leaving behind them no initial or overt signs of their attack; furthermore, it is the
basic premise of this tale's central episode that the witches are unable to attack
a body that is directly watched (Motif J).

Finally, let us turn to an episode from the beginning of the novel. Here one
Aristomenes tells of his attempt to rescue his friend Socrates from the enslaving
clutches of Meroe, innkeeper and witch, and bring him safely away from
Thessaly. At this point Meroe, together with her sidekick Panthia (the Sagana
to her Canidia) has tracked the fugitive pair down to another inn, in which they
are resting for the night:

> But I shut the door, made the bolts fast, and pushed my pallet-bed tight up
> behind the hinge, and laid myself upon it. To start with I was awake for quite
> a while because of my fear. Then, at around the third watch [of the night]
> I managed to shut my eyes for a bit. I had only just got off the sleep when the
> doors suddenly flew open with greater force than you would have thought
> robbers could muster. Indeed they were actually broken open, torn right out of
> their hinge-sockets and flung onto the floor. My pallet-bed, which was an
> insubstantial thing anyway, rotten and with one leg too short, was also flung
> forward by the strength of the force used. I was thrown out of it, but it landed
> back on top of me upside down, and covered me and hid me. . . . Down there in
> the dirt, I looked out sideways to see what was going on, shrewdly shielded by
> my bed. I saw two rather old women. One was carrying a bright lamp, the other
> a sponge and an unsheathed sword. With this paraphernalia they stood over
> Socrates, who was still fast asleep. . . . Meroe pushed Socrates' head to one side
> and plunged the whole sword into the left side of his neck, right up to the hilt.
> She applied a little leather bottle to his neck and carefully caught up the blood
> that welled out, so that there was not a drop to be seen anywhere. I saw this with

---

[138] Van Mal-Maeder 2001: 307–95 offers a detailed commentary on this episode; cf. also
Frangoulidis 2008, esp. 85–107 and Cherubini 2010a: 37–8.

my own eyes. Because, I believe, the good lady Meroe did not wish to depart in any way from sacrificial observance, she stuck her right hand into the wound and, delving down to his innards, probed about and pulled my poor companion's heart out. With that Socrates brought forth a noise, or rather an indistinct screech [*stridor*], through the wound in his throat that the sword had hacked open, and gurgled out his last breath. Panthia used the sponge to stop up the wound at its widest point and said, 'Now, sponge, born in the sea, cross not over a river!' . . . They had just stepped through the doorway when the doors leaped back into position, undamaged. The hinge-axles slotted back into their sockets, the bars returned to the posts, and the bolts ran back to do their locking . . . .
Apuleius *Metamorphoses* 1.11–14

Despite all he has witnessed, Aristomenes eventually discovers that Socrates remains alive. In the morning the two men accordingly continue with their journey of escape, and Aristomenes dismisses the terrible experiences of the preceding night as a drunken dream:

'You're raving', I said to myself. 'You were deep in your cups and had a bizarre dream. See, Socrates is safe, sound, and unharmed. Where's the wound? Where's the sponge? Where, indeed, is the scar, which went so deep, and is so new?' Apuleius *Metamorphoses* 1.18

Then the two men pause to take a meal beside a river:

But when Socrates had chomped through enough food, he was seized by an unbearable thirst. He had, after all, greedily gulped down a healthy helping of excellent cheese. Not far from the roots of the plane tree there dawdled a small stream, as calm as a pool, and looking like silver or glass. 'See', I said, 'refresh yourself with the milky water from this spring.' He rose to his feet and found a place where the bank had an even edge. Then he got down on his knees and brought himself close to the water in his eagerness to get a drink. He had hardly touched the water's surface with the tips of his lips, when his throat-wound yawned open and deep, and the sponge suddenly bounced out of it, followed by just a bit of blood. Then his lifeless corpse almost fell headlong into the river, but I managed to hold onto one of his feet and, with an effort, drag him back up the bank. Once there, I wept over the poor little man, as much as I could under the circumstances, and covered him with the sandy earth. He will lie forever beside that river. Apuleius *Metamorphoses* 1.19[139]

Here again we find a number of the motifs of a *strix* attack refracted. First of all, we find the witches having to resort to trickery, to magic indeed, to get past a normal locked door in order to attack their victims within. They magically burst the door from its hinge – as becomes particularly clear when they magically restore it to its locked position as they leave. It may be salient too that Apuleius

---

[139] For commentaries see Scobie 1975 and Keulen 2007; cf. also Frangoulidis 2008: 46–68.

draws attention to the door-hinge itself in all this, this perhaps being a typical point of entry for *striges* adopting the soul-flying technique (Motifs D, F). Secondly, Meroe removes from Socrates a vital organ, his heart. Perhaps we may view the sponge as a substitute heart, in parallel with the wax prostheses used by the Thelyphron witches to make good, on a temporary basis, the body parts they had stolen (Motif H). Thirdly, in doing this she contrives to invade and raid his body surreptitiously, with her brutal work leaving no visible wound in his throat (Motif J). Fourthly, Meroe also drains Socrates of his moisture, catching up all his blood bar a few drops in a little leather bottle (*utriculus*) – and clearly there is yet more magic afoot here too, since a little bottle could hardly have the capacity to receive the expected 12 pints (Motif I). Fifthly, she imposes a time-limit on Socrates' life, destining him in her incantation for death at the point at which he passes over a river (Motif K). Sixthly, we even find appeal made to the screech: the noise Socrates emits from his wounded throat is described with the term *stridor*, the noun cognate with *stridere* (Motif E).

Meroe is, furthermore, possessed of a gruesome repertoire beyond this. She can raise ghosts and open up the underworld.[140] She has transformed another errant lover into a beaver so that, as the animal supposedly does, he will gnaw off his own genitals. When insulted by the wife of another of her lovers, she had put a binding spell on her then pregnant womb; now, nine years later, her belly is distended by the full-sized eight-year-old child it continues to carry.[141]

None of these episodes explicitly features *striges*, to make the point again, although Aristomenes does describe Meroe and Panthia explicitly as *lamias*.[142] But these episodes have clearly been shaped to refract the *strix*-paradigm and to incorporate and re-articulate some of its striking motifs. The attention given to the need for witches to deploy magical means to overcome locked doors in both the cases of Meroe and the Thelyphron witches is particularly striking, as is the attention given to the hinge-gap in the Pamphile tale and the chink in the wall in the Thelyphron tale. These details seem to mesh particularly well with the John Damascene passage and thereby, valuably, give indirect but nonetheless strong confirmation that the *strix* culture represented in it is truly ancient and not some recent and independent Byzantine invention.

3.6 Augustine's Italian Landladies

In his *c.* AD 420 *City of God* Augustine has some interesting things to tell us about some Italian witches who, like Apuleius' Meroe, also doubled as innkeepers:

[140] Apuleius *Metamorphoses* 1.8.   [141] Apuleius *Metamorphoses* 1.9.
[142] Apuleius *Metamorphoses* 1.17.

For we too, when we were in Italy, used to hear such things about a particular district of those parts, where it was said that women that kept inns, imbued with these evil crafts, used to give things in cheese to such travellers as they wished, or as they were able to, as a result of which they were immediately turned into beasts of burden, made to carry whatever was demanded and to return to their own form again once they had performed their tasks. But their minds did not become those of beasts, but were preserved in their rational and human state, just as Apuleius told or pretended happened to himself [*sic*] in the books that he wrote under the title of *The Golden Ass* [= *Metamorphoses*], namely that after taking a drug he became an ass but retained his human mind. ... A man called Praestantius told that this happened to his father, namely that he consumed that drug in some cheese in his own house, and lay on his bed as if asleep, although he could in no way be roused. He said that he returned to consciousness after a certain number of days and told the story of what he had experienced as if recounting dreams. He said that he had become a pack-horse indeed, and had, in the company of other beasts of burden, carried supplies for the soldiers of the so-called Rhetian legion, since it was being dispatched to Rhetia. It was discovered that this had happened, just as he recounted it, even though these things had seemed to be dreams to him.

Augustine *City of God* 18.18

The link with the *strix*-paradigm here is a single and indirect one, but nonetheless intriguing. As emerges, the witch-innkeepers are held to put their victims into a catatonic state and project their souls from them to serve them as beasts of burden (Augustine is understandably troubled by the notion that insubstantial souls should have the ability to lift physical burdens, and proceeds to offer the Christianising explanation that the actual lifting is undertaken by demons). This rare association of witches with soul-projection perhaps salutes the particular abilities of the *strix*, even if in this case the soul-flight is an experience the witch imposes upon others as opposed to undertaking herself (Motif D).

3.7 The Witches of Burchard of Worms

The *strix*-paradigm is saluted in a quite striking and dense way in a brief passage of Burchard of Worms' *c.* AD 1012–20 *Corrector* sive *Medicus*, as the nineteenth book of his *Decrees* is known:

[N] Have you come to believe [A] what many women that have turned to Satan believe and declare to be true? [B] Do you believe that, in the silence of a disturbed night, when you have put yourself to bed and your husband lies in your embrace, [F] you are able to depart through closed doors, for all that you have a bodily form? [D] That you have the power to travel considerable distances over the world, together with other women in the grip of a similar delusion? [J] That, without any visible weapons, you have the power to kill people that have been baptized and redeemed by the blood of Christ? **[H, I]** That you have the power to cook their flesh and devour them and to substitute their heart with straw or wood, or something else of this sort? **[J, K]** That you have the power to restore them to life after you have eaten them, and allow them to live for a limited reprieve? **[N]** If that is what you have come to believe, you should do penance for forty days, that is a diet of bread and water only, for forty days, for a series of seven years.

Burchard of Worms *Decretorum libri xx* 19.5, *PL* cxl, col. 973[143]

Burchard's sceptical vignette of a witch at work by night (Motifs A, B) cleaves particularly closely to the *strix*-paradigm, and for this reason we have integrated motif-tags into the text as quoted; indeed, were it not for the fact that it does not explicitly deploy the term *strix*, we would have given it the status of a fourth principal text in Section 1. The phrase 'That you have the power to travel considerable distances over the world' archly salutes the notion of flight (Motif D). The phrase 'you are able to depart through closed doors, for all that you have a bodily form' more particularly salutes the notion of soul-flight, as well as the ever-concomitant problem of how a disembodied soul might be able to make a physical impact on the tangible world (Motif F). The following phrase, 'without any visible weapons, you have the power to kill people', makes a similar point whilst also saluting the notion of invisibility more directly (Motif J). The phrase 'you have the power to cook their flesh and devour them and to substitute their heart with straw or wood' salutes the theme of body-part theft (Motif H) and perhaps too, in its reference to straw, that of moisture-extraction (Motif I). The phrase 'That you have the power to restore them to life after you have eaten them, and allow them to live for a limited reprieve?' explicitly salutes the theme of the surreptitious and debilitating attack (Motif J), as well as directly asserting the notion of the application of a fixed limit to life (Motif K). And the vignette as a whole is presented as an item of foolish, female folk-belief (Motif N). For all that it does not mention the term *strix*, and for all its lateness, this text is of particular value for the fact that – much like the Apuleian material – it aligns so tightly with the John Damascene passage, and demonstrates that the details of particular interest in it, especially those relating to soul-flight and the problem of house penetration, are no oddities peculiar to the Greek tradition, but belong equally in the heart of the Latin one.

3.8 Conclusion

The impact of the *strix*-paradigm on the general representation of witches in Latin literature is clear. A great many of the witches not explicitly defined as

---

[143] Cf. Cherubini 2010a: 41, 68–9, 75, 2010b: 68–9.

striges nonetheless borrow features and feels from them. And we may surmise that the Latin witch's more general characteristics of gruesome morbidity and devotion to the macabre and body horror are to be ascribed to the spreading stain of the *strix*-paradigm.

I return to a question I have posed before, and venture to answer it with greater precision. Students of the ancient magical tradition are always struck by a contrast between the representation of witches in the Greek tradition and those in the Latin one. Some of the witches of the Greek tradition can even appear relatively harmless. One thinks of Theocritus' Simaetha, discovered in the course of making a complex love spell – something of an amateur, admittedly.[144] Others are terrible and dangerous. The very first witch of the Greek tradition, Homer's Circe, is inscrutable, cruel and a virtual cannibal: she mercilessly turns visitors to her island into animals, and those she transforms into pigs she presumably proposes to eat (for what other purposes do pigs have?).[145] And they can be violent too: the second witch of the Greek tradition, Medea, masterminds the killing of her brother Apsyrtus, and the hacking off of his extremities;[146] similarly she hacks up the bodies of Aeson, Jason and Pelias, albeit in the course of rejuvenating them by boiling them up with her special herbs in her cauldron (in the case of the wicked Pelias, however, the key ingredient is omitted . . .);[147] she butchers her own children whilst burning her love-rival Glauce to death, and her father too, with a poison wedding dress.[148] Nonetheless, neither Circe nor Medea, in their Greek manifestations, possesses this distinctive quality of the Roman witch that I have here defined as 'gruesome morbidity', and which in previous work I referred to as 'the Gothic'.

So why this distinctive difference? Whence this 'gruesome morbidity' of the Roman witch? Previously, I took refuge in a general appeal to the Roman sensibility – the sensibility of the amphitheatre, with its beast shows and gladiators, in which the Roman public was ever more inured to the sight of human innards flopping into the sand.[149] And this is not an explanation from which I now resile: it remains valid enough at its rather abstract level. But I now suggest in addition this more immediate cause for the distinctive character of the

---

[144] Theocritus *Idylls* 2.
[145] Homer *Odyssey* 10. For those that continue to doubt that Circe is a witch: Ogden 2021, Appendix A.
[146] Apollonius of Rhodes *Argonautica* 4.452–80, etc.
[147] Aeson: *Nostoi* F6 West. Jason: Simonides F548 *PMG*, Pherecydes F113 Fowler. Pelias: Pindar *Pythians* 4.249–50, Pherecydes F105 Fowler, Euripides *Peliades* (*TrGF*), Apollonius of Rhodes *Argonautica* 4.241–3, Diodorus 4.50–2, Apollodorus *Bibliotheca* 1.9.27.
[148] Eumelus F23, Euripides *Medea* 1136–1291, Diodorus 4.54, Apollodorus *Bibliotheca* 1.9.28.
[149] Ogden 2008: 75–6.

Roman witch: the integration of the *strix*-paradigm into her representation, and its pervasive effects upon her repertoire.[150]

4 The Longue Durée: Greece and the Near East

The *strix* is a woman with exceptional powers, not a demon, but she otherwise fits tightly into a long tradition of belief in child-killing demons that can be traced from second-millennium BC Mesopotamia to the Greek world of the nineteenth century AD.

4.1 Mesopotamian Lamashtu and Gallû

The work of the demon Lamashtu is clearly conveyed in a series of Akkadian texts of the second and first millennia BC, which I here excerpt:

- **A xxi–xvi BC text from Babylon:** 'Her hands are little, her fingers are very long, her elbows are dirty. She enters through the door of the house, she slips in past the door-pivot, she has slipped in past the door-pivot, she kills the little ones; she has given it (the child) a seizure in its abdomen seven times . . . you must go away.'
- **A xiii–xii BC text from Ugarit:** 'Daily she counts the days of pregnant females, she pursues those giving birth. "Bring me your sons, that I may suckle them, and your daughters, that I may raise them." . . . She enters the open house, she sneaks in by the door of the closed house. You have never ceased absorbing the blood of humans . . . the flesh that one must not eat, the bone that one must not crush (?) . . . I exorcise you . . . .'
- **The first-millennium *Lamashtu Text* from Nineveh and elsewhere:** 'Goddess whose face is fearful . . . By the name of the great gods enchanted, with the birds of the sky fly away . . . Go away, remove yourself and fly away from the body of this child . . . You drink the blood . . . of men, (their) flesh, that is not for eating, their bones, that are not for nibbling . . . she sweeps the innards of pregnant women, violently she tears the child out of the pregnant . . . serpents in the hands . . . Great is Anu's daughter, who torments the little ones.'

---

[150] Cf. Frankfurter 2014: 323: 'The common picture in Greco-Roman literature of a lascivious older woman who uses barbaric utterances and nocturnal rites to bind some unwitting youth reflected . . . not a real social type but rather the folklore of the night-witch – *strix, gello,* or *lilith* – who eats children and drains men's potency.' Indeed, but it is misleading to conflate Greek and Roman traditions in this way: only in Greek texts that are late and manifestly post-Latin could the *strix*-paradigm be said to make a significant impact on broader witch-portrayal – as, for example, in the case of (the iv AD?) Heliodorus' old woman of Bessa (*Aethiopica* 6.12–15).

• **A first-millennium BC text from Uruk:** 'Her hair is in disorder, her breasts are uncovered . . . her hands are in the flesh and the blood; she enters by the window, she glides like a serpent; she enters the house, she leaves the house: "Bring me your children, that I may suckle them, and your little girls, that I may be their guardian; to the mouth of your little girls I want to give the breast."'[151]

Lamashtu is depicted on a *c.* 800–500 BC stone amulet from Carchemish. Here she has the head of a lion; the torso of a human female, with a boar and a jackal hanging from her breasts; the legs of a bird, with which she stands on a donkey, symbolically carrying her off to a place she can do no harm; and she brandishes a pair of snakes in her human arms.[152]

The motifs familiar from the *strix*-paradigm stand out clearly: flying (Motifs C, D); penetration of the protective house (Motif F), including surreptitious penetration by means of any tiny aperture, especially the hinge-gap (Motif F); the devouring of children (Motifs G, H); the extraction of moisture (Motif I); the surreptitious infiltration of the child's body, including by means of giving it suck and a perverted variety of foster-mothering (Motif J).

Mesopotamia knew of another deadly demon with a broader remit, Gallû: 'The evil *gallû*-demon roams in the city, he kills people without mercy.'[153] The analogue here is less pressing, not least because Gallû is male, though the fact that he operates by night (Motif B) is suggestive. But his importance lies in the fact that he was to be swept up into Greek culture alongside Lamashtu, where he was transformed into a female demon Gello, and assimilated more closely to her.

4.2 Greek Lamia and Gello

Lamia, Greek culture's reflex of Lamashtu, is a complex and contradictory figure.[154] Sometimes we encounter a single demonic entity with Lamia as a proper name. In this case she has a back-story. As Duris of Samos tells (*c.* 280 BC):

Lamia was a beautiful woman in Libya. Zeus had sex with her. Because of Hera's envy towards her she lost [*or*: destroyed] the children she bore.

---

[151] Translations taken from West 1995: 250–9, 276–7; cf. also Farber 1983, 1989, West 1991, Burkert 1992: 82–7, McDonough 1997: 335–6, Wiggermann 2000.
[152] London, British Museum no. 117759; for an illustration see, e.g., Burkert 1992 fig. 5.
[153] The text is given at West 1995: 313, with others along similar lines.
[154] For general discussion of Lamia and Gello, see Boardman 1992, Burkert 1992: 82–7, Spier 1993, Leinweber 1994, Johnston 1995, 1999: 161–99, Resnick and Kitchell 2007, Viltanioti 2012, Ingemark and Ingemark 2013, Patera 2015 (a detailed study), Björklund 2017a, Eidinow 2018.

Consequently, she became misshapen through grief, snatched other people's children and killed them.'   Duris of Samos *FGrH/BNJ* 76 F17[155]

At other times we encounter a plural phenomenon, with *lamia* now as a categorical term. These plural *lamias* are sometimes presented as demons again or as apparitions, but at other times rather as terrible beasts.[156] Sometimes such *lamias* similarly pursue and devour children, to whom they are presented as bogeys,[157] but at other times they pursue and devour rather young men.[158] Sometimes too they retain Lamashtu's serpentine element, which the scholarship on them has tended to neglect.[159] Let us briefly consider a single example here, the *lamia* of a Greek myth better preserved in the Latin tradition. When the Argives anger the god Apollo for having allowed his former lover Psamathe and their child Linus to die, he takes his revenge on the city by sending against it:

a monster conceived in the deepest part of the Acheron, in the Furies' unspeakable halls. The monster had the face and breast of a girl but from her head there rose a snake [*anguis*], hissing continuously, parting her ruddy forehead. Then this dread blight slid into rooms by night with scaly gait [i.e., her bottom half also consisted of a snake], snatched newborn souls from the bosoms of their nurses, devoured them with bloody bite and grew fat on the grief of the land.   Statius *Thebaid* 1.597–604 (*c.* AD 92)

When the monster's eventual killer, Coroebus, first encounters her, this is the scene with which he is confronted:

The bodies of two small children hung by her side, and already her hooked hand was fast in their guts and her iron-shod talons were growing warm in their soft hearts. Statius *Thebaid* 1.609–11[160]

---

[155] For other sources, which may or may not bear upon the same individual, see Crates *Lamia* F20 K-A; Aristophanes *Wasps* 1035 and *Peace* 758 (with scholl.); Plutarch *De Pythiae oraculis* 9 (*Moralia* 398c); Pausanias 10.12.1; Clement of Alexandria *Stromateis* 1.15.70; Photius *Lexicon* s. v. Λάμια (62).

[156] On the demon or apparition side, see Philostratus *Life of Apollonius* 4.25; Hesychius *s.vv.* λάμιαι. On the beast side, see Antoninus Liberalis *Metamorphoses* 8 Lamia (paraphrasing Nicander); Diodorus 20.41.2–6, Hesychius s.v. *Lamia*; Photius *Lexicon* s.v. Λάμια (60); and (possibly) Dionysius of Halicarnassus *On Thucydides* 6.

[157] Diodorus 20.41.2–6; Horace *Ars Poetica* 340; Statius *Thebaid* 1.562–669; Isidore of Seville *Etymologies* 8.11.102; *Suda* s.v. Μορμώ.

[158] Dio Chrysostom *Orations* 5; Antoninus Liberalis *Metamorphoses* 8 Lamia; Philostratus *Life of Apollonius* 4.25; Heraclitus *De incredibilibus* 34 Lamia.

[159] Dio Chrysostom *Orations* 5; Statius *Thebaid* 1.562–669; Antoninus Liberalis *Metamorphoses* 8 Lamia; Philostratus *Life of Apollonius* 4.25. But see now Ogden 2013: 86–92 and (forthcoming), ch. 3.

[160] Statius does not explicitly define this wonderful creature as a *lamia*, but the term is found in the reference to the episode at First Vatican Mythographer 2.66 Zorzetti. An image of this creature is to be found already on a V BC Athenian white-ground *lekythos*: *LIMC* Apollon 998 = Python 2 (where it is misattributed to Python; see Ogden 2013: 87–8).

In the texts we have examined above the affinity between *lamias* and *striges* is recognised implicitly by Apuleius – when he has his Aristomenes describe the *strix*-like witches Meroe and Panthia as *lamiae* – and explicitly by Gervase of Tilbury.[161] It is recognised too in an Aristides scholiast's description of the single Libyan Lamia as a *strigla* (for which see the following section).[162]

Gello is attested more poorly, but earlier. Already in *c.* 600 BC Sappho used the grimly ironic proverb 'more child-loving than Gello'. Zenobius (ii AD), preserving her proverb, explains that, for the inhabitants of ancient Lesbos, she had been a girl that had died before her time, still a virgin, and that she went on to attack children as an apparition (*phantasma*), with the further deaths of those that died before their time consequently being ascribed to her.[163] The *Cyranides* (iv AD?) speaks of her as a suffocater of new-borns and of mothers in childbed.[164]

As we have seen, John Damascene knows that, just as there are plural *lamiai*, so there are plural – in the form of the term he uses – *geloudes*. But for him these are not now a demon category, but actually the same thing as *striges*. Subsequently the xi AD Michael Psellus was to regard Gello (whom he knows as Gillo) and the *striges* as distinct but interchangeable phenomena:

> At any rate, [*sc.* the author of the secret Hebrew book, *The Solomon*] says that Gillo kills embryonic babies, all the ones that slip from the womb. The period of her killing is defined as a year.[165] ... But the prevailing opinion these days ascribes this ability to old hags [*graïdia*]. It provides them with wings and sends them unseen into children's houses. Then it has these women suckle the children and themselves suck all the, as it were, moisture out of them. At any rate, the women that attend childbirth call the newborns that waste away 'Gillo-devoured' [*Gillobrōta*].
>
> Michael Psellus *Opuscula psychologica, theologica, daemonologica* 164 [*De Gillo*][166]

---

[161] Apuleius *Metamorphoses* 1.17; Gervase of Tilbury *Otia imperiala* 3.86 (pp. 39–40 Liebrecht).
[162] Schol. Aristides *Panathenaicus* 102 (iii p. 42 Dindorf).
[163] Zenobius *Proverbs* 1.58, incorporating Sappho F168a Voigt.
[164] *Cyranides* 2.40.35–38; see also Hesychius *s.vv.* Γελ(λ)ώ, Γελλῶς and *Suda* s.v. Γελλοῦς παιδοφιλωτέρα.
[165] I.e., babies dying within their first twelve months are held to have been killed by her.
[166] The translation of this passage offered at West 1995: 311–12 is misleading in a number of respects, the points about house-penetration and moisture in particular being mishandled. However, West may, just conceivably, be right in reading the two penultimate sentences as referring to the agency not of a strikingly active 'prevailing opinion' but to that of Gillo herself: in other words, it is she that furnishes the hags with their wings and compels them to suckle, etc. That the demon should be seen as the patron and controller of the witches in this way is a fascinating prospect. But this reading: (a) undervalues the disjunctive force of the initial ἀλλά; (b) assumes a difficult unmarked change of subject between παρέχεται and πτεροῖ; and (c) then again undervalues the force of the sense-break indicated by γοῦν, as we return to the subject of Gillo herself as a devourer.

The word is not used, but we cannot doubt that Psellus' hags here are precisely *striges*: they are old (Motif A); they fly (Motif C); they can make themselves invisible (Motif D) and slip surreptitiously into houses (Motif F); they suckle babies (Motif J) and they drain them of their moisture (Motif I).

In the case of Gallû–Gello the 'longue durée' is very long indeed. A charm against 'Ghelou' was still being copied as late as the turn of the twentieth century AD. The charm incorporates a so-called *historiola*, a 'little paradigmatic story', the action of which it aspires to replicate, albeit in this case the story is quite an expansive one. The story speaks of the demon's ultimate defeat at the hands of St Sisinnos as she had attempted to take Melitene's child. The means by which she had surreptitiously entered the woman's house here is intriguing: she had disguised herself as a clod of earth stuck to a horse's shoe.[167]

Traces survive of a third demon of this same type, Mormo. The scholia to Aristides give her a vestigial aetiological story resembling Lamia's, with the comparison being made explicitly:

> 'The things that terrify children when they hear them' refers to Mormo and Lamia . . . . Mormo was a Corinthian woman. She devoured her own children and then in the evening flew up into the sky for some reason. So now, when women want to scare their children, they shout 'Mormo!' Theocritus has 'Mormo bites!' This is the origin of the deterrent bogies [*mormolykia*].
>
> schol. Aelius Aristides *Panathenaicus* 102.5 (iii p. 42 Dindorf)

To return once more to our *strix* motif-set, we note that, like the *strix*, Mormo both devours children (Motifs G, H) and, somehow, flies (Motifs C, D). The Theocritean scholia commenting on the proverb cited here (in context it is deployed by a mother to deter her baby from getting too close to a horse's teeth) go so far as to make a three-way comparison between Mormo, Lamia and Gello.[168]

4.3 Was There a Greek *Strix* Before the Roman One?

This deep historical context of child-killing demons urges a fundamental question upon us: Was there a Greek *strix* before the Roman one? It is, alas, impossible to be sure, and this uncertainty begins with the language of origin of the term itself. Modern etymologists do, however, generally believe that it originated in Latin before migrating into Greek, as opposed to vice versa.[169] We

---

[167] For the Melitene text see Gaster 1900, esp. 143–9, Argenti and Rose 1949: 42–5, Greenfield 1988, Viltanioti 2012, Patera 2016: 157–64 and Björklund 2017c: 350–1.

[168] Theocritus *Idylls* 15.40, with scholl. Cf. also Erinna F1b.26–27 Diehl (here she is described as big-eared, four-footed and shape-shifting), *Suda* s.vv. μορμολύκεια, μορμολύττεται, Μορμώ. Discussion at Patera 2015: 106–44.

[169] Frisk 1960–72 and Chantraine 2008 *s.v.* στρίγξ cautiously prefer the Latin origin; Beekes 2010 *s.v.* στρί(γ)ξ remains agnostic; de Vaan 2008 oddly accords the term no entry.

can make four observations: (a) the term is first attested in Latin two centuries before it is attested in Greek; (b) the evidence for the term in Greek is scrappy until we come to the key John Damascene passage; (c) the verbal instability of the term in Greek, which far exceeds its instability in Latin, may suggest that it was not originally resident in the language; and (d) there is nothing in the Greek evidence for the *strix*, such as it is, to suggest that a Greek *strix* differed in any way from the Roman paradigm, although the *striglos* that eventually developed out of it is clearly a rather different entity.

Table 2 lays out the first attestations, so far as I am able to trace them, of *strix*-related terms in Greek, with further attestations of them, such as they are, being merely repetitive of the same severely restricted range of content.[170]

Let us give a little further attention to the question of the term's very first attestation in Greek, and then to the chronology of the development of the distinctive variant term *striglos*. As we have seen, the earliest attestation of the term *strix* in Latin comes in the early-second-century BC comic playwright Plautus' *Pseudolus*. All Plautus' Latin comedies based their plots on Greek originals of the fourth or third centuries BC (the specific original behind the *Pseudolus* is unknown),[171] but not so their superficial comic business, so there is no strong reason to suppose that his *striges* originated in the unidentified source play.

By contrast, the earliest certain Greek attestation (and the only one with any significant content prior to the John Damascene text) for any of the relevant Greek forms comes in the brief folksong fragment discussed in Section 2.3: 'Send away the *strinx*, the long-eared-owl-*strinx*, from people, the bird that should not be named, onto swift-faring ships.' This is recorded by the later-second-century AD grammarian Festus, but his quotation of it falls within an outer quotation of another Roman grammarian, the Augustan Verrius Flaccus. So we can say that the folksong was current in the Augustan era, but we have no way of knowing how much older it may be than that. The apotropaic content

---

[170] For the sake of completeness, let us note some further Greek texts of interest which do not, however, deploy a *strix* term. (a) The name of Greek literature's foundational witch, the Homeric Circe (*Kirkē*), is thought to derive from *kirkos* ('hawk'), although the *Odyssey* makes nothing of this: see Yarnall 1994: 28–35, Marinatos 2000: 32–45. For the witch-as-raptor as a folktale motif more generally, see Thompson 1955–8 G211. (b) As we have seen, the originally Hellenistic *Lapidary of Damigeron-Evax* (28.1, at Halleux and Schamp 1985: 266–7) prescribes an amulet against *nyktalōpes*, 'creatures that see by night'; the v–vi AD Latin adaptation glosses this term with, inter alia, *striges*, but it seems unlikely that the Greek original had offered a parallel gloss: see Halleux and Schamp's commentary. (c) Just as Apuleius seemingly makes appeal to the *strix*-paradigm in his account of witch Pamphile's transformation into a (non-*strix*) owl at *Metamorphoses* 3.21, the Greek model for this text, reflected in summary form in the *Onos* (12), can be seen to have done the same (see Section 3.5). (d) The (xi AD) Michael Psellus text just considered, *Opuscula psychologica, theologica, daemonologica* 164 [*De Gillo*], seems to speak precisely of *striges* whilst falling short of using the term.

[171] Duckworth 1952: 52.

Table 2 *Strix* terminology in Greek: first attestations

Singular	Plural	Date of first attestation	Source of first attestation	Observations
strinx *σπρίγξ*	*stringes* *σπρίγγες*	turn of the eras or before	Festus p. 414 Lindsay, quoting the Augustan Verrius Flaccus, in turn quoting an existing Greek folksong, 859 Campbell	Folksong fragment reads: 'Send away the *strinx*, the long-eared-owl-*strinx*, from people, the bird that should not be named, onto swift-faring ships'; Aelius Herodianus (see next row) defines as 'a kind of bird' only.
strix *σπρίξ*	*striges* *σπρίγες*	ii AD	Aelius Herodianus *De prosodia catholica* p. 396 Lentz	The grammarian defines as 'a kind of bird' only.
stlix *σπλίξ*	*stliges* *σπλίγες*	"	"	"
stryx *σπρύξ*	*stryges* *σπρύγες*	"	"	May be erroneous: the grammarian cites the word without defining it.

Word	Date	Source	
styx στύξ/ στῦξ *styges *στύγες/ *στῦγες	ii–iii AD (iv BC?)	Antoninus Liberalis *Metamorphoses* 21 (ii–iii AD), reworking the iv BC Boio?	'For Antoninus (and Boio?) the term signifies 'bat'; for Hesychius *s.v.* (c. AD 600) it means 'little horned owl' (*skōps*).
strigla στρίγλα *striglai *στρίγλαι	iv–x AD	scholia to Aelius Aristides, p.102 Jebb	'Lamia ... speaking colloquially [*idiōtikōs*] we would now call her a *strigla*.'
striglos στρίγλος *strigloi *στρίγλοι	c. AD 600	Hesychius *s.v.*	' ... night-wanderer; it is also called the "little owl" [*nyktoboa*]; according to others, the "long-eared owl" [*nyktikorax*]'
*strynga *στρύγξ *stryngai στρύγγαι	c. AD 700?	John Damascene *De draconibus et strygibus, PG* 94, 1604	Dating depends on the fragment being genuinely ascribed to John Damascene

suggests that the *strinx* in question is at least broadly conceptualised along the same lines as the Latin *strix*.

This picture is potentially complicated by the variant form – if such it is – *styx*, as found in (the ii–iii AD) Antoninus Liberalis. Like Plautus, Antoninus bases his material on that of an earlier Greek text, in this case the lost fourth-century BC *Ornithogoniae* of Boio. It is admittedly quite likely that Boio himself deployed this same term (the chances of a direct reflection are rather better here than they are in the case of Plautus and his models). However, the context in Antoninus' story suggests that the term *styx* here signifies not any sort of owl or owl-like witch, but actually a bat.[172] Antoninus tells how, after Polyphonte had failed to give honour to Aphrodite, the goddess turned her mad, whereupon she coupled with a bear and gave birth to a pair of wild, bear-like, cannibalistic sons. The three of them were at once punished and saved when Ares and Hermes transformed them into 'birds'.[173] These are the words in which Antoninus describes the transformation of Polyphonte herself: 'Polyphonte became a *styx*: it calls out by night; it does not eat or drink; it holds its head down and the tips of its feet up; it is a harbinger of war and civil strife for men.'[174] On this basis we must assume that we are dealing with a separate word. The fact that the form *styx* is the only one of all the (potential) variants in Greek and Latin to lack the liquid consonant (*r* or *l*) after the initial *st-* also gives serious pause for thought.[175] Accordingly, we are justified in excluding the form *styx* from the *strix*-family.

But there is then a further complication: the *c.* AD 600 lexicographer Hesychius subsequently affirms that the term *styx* signifies a variety of owl, specifically a little horned owl (*skōps*). I suspect, nonetheless, that the term *styx* is less an owl than a cuckoo in the nest. I suggest that Hesychius does not actually know what it means and that, having come across it – probably in a text other than Boio's or Antoninus', where its context was less clear – he has conjectured a meaning for it under the influence of *strix*. In short, it has still

---

[172] A point well made by Oliphant 1913: 133–5. Nonetheless, he does indeed wish to include *styx* within the set of *strix* terms and even contends (136) that Titinius' words on the *strix* also entail that it is a bat, given that his *strix* has nipples (F ex incertis fabulis xxii Ribbeck, quoted in Section 2) and that Ovid's words do likewise (141–2 n.19). But it is important to note that Pliny effectively differentiates the *strix* from the bat at *Natural History* 11.232 (also quoted in Section 2). Cf. McDonough 1997: 326, Cherubini 2009b: 89, 2010b: 74 n.4.

[173] We have noted above the understandable ancient propensity to classify bats as 'birds': Section 2.3.

[174] For commentaries, see Celoria 1992 and Papathomopoulos 2002 *ad loc.*

[175] Cherubini 2010a: 76–95 (cf. 2009b: 79 n.7, 89, 2010b: 71, 74) builds much on the assumption that this form does indeed belong in the set whilst, however, holding the form *stlix* to be spurious (2010a: 14); but see Oliphant 2014: 57 ('lallation').

to be demonstrated that any Greek term legitimately belónging to the *strix*-family is attested, directly or indirectly, prior to the Latin *strix*.

Of the various forms preserved by the second-century AD Aelius Herodianus only *stryx* (*stryges*) calls for comment. This is the one term in his set for which he does not supply a meaning, and so it may be wholly irrelevant. However, the bilingual *Glossary of Philoxenus*, preserved in a ix AD manuscript, glosses, as we have seen, the Latin term *striga* in Greek not only as 'a witch woman' (*gynē pharmakis*) but also as 'a Laestrygonian'.[176] The linkage with Homer's Laestrygonians is not completely absurd: this giant race did, after all, eat people.[177] But the fact that the glossary can make the link to them – and it is probably an implicit claim to etymology – may suggest that it knew of a form of the word *strix* with the root *stryg-*.

Let us turn now to *striglos* and *strigla*. Hesychius' lexicon offers the following definition of the term *striglos*, the sole attestation of this specific formulation:

> *striglos*: the inside of a horn/wing; 'night-wanderer'; it is also called 'the little owl' [*nyktoboa*, lit. 'night-shouter']; according to others, 'the long-eared owl' [*nyktikorax*, lit. 'night-crow].[178]

Although *striglos*-as-inside-of-a-horn/wing and *striglos*-as-owl share a lemma in Hesychius' lexicon, they are presumably homophones rather than truly the same word. However, given the radical difference between the first definition and the following ones here, it has been conjectured that some words have fallen out of the lexicon's textual tradition, and that all definitions except the first belonged to a lost intervening lemma, namely the more familiar *strinx*. In other words, the lexicon would originally have offered something along the following lines:

> *striglos*: the inside of a horn/wing < . . .
> *strinx*: . . . 'they call the *strinx* "the> night-wanderer"; it is also called "the little owl"; according to others, "the long-eared owl".'[179]

---

[176] *Glossary of Philoxenus* s.v. *striga*.

[177] Homer *Odyssey* 10.76–132. They also inhabit 'the city of Lǎmos' (81), the name of which might be held to evoke 'Lǎmia'. Cf. Oliphant 1914: 51–2.

[178] We need not infer that the *striglos* is a male *strix*, even though words of the second declension ending in -*os* are more commonly masculine and male-related.

[179] I.e.: στρίγλος· τὰ ἐντὸς τοῦ κέρατος < . . . στρίγξ· . . . 'στρίγγα> νυκτίφοιτον'. καλεῖται δὲ καὶ νυκτοβόα. οἱ δὲ νυκτικόρακα. Cf. Hansen's 2005 edition *ad loc*. One might think that the phrase τὰ ἐντὸς τοῦ κέρατος ought to signify the core of animal's horn. However, the iv AD Latin grammarian Charisius' gloss on the term *strix* (NB) explains that this form at any rate bore a technical military sense in which it signified 'the gap between cavalry squadrons in which the horses are pressed together [*stringuntur*]' (*Ars grammatica*, i p. 109 Keil); the deeply corrupt Festus p. 414 Lindsay, in a passage immediately preceding the one quoted above, can be

The suggestion is a clever one, but it falls doubly foul of Occam's razor. Firstly, we know from a scholium to Aristides that Greek developed a parallel first-declension variant of *striglos* in a *strix*-associated sense. After rehearsing the content of the Duris fragment on Lamia, the scholium observes, 'Speaking colloquially [*idiōtikōs*] we would now call her a *strigla*.'[180] Alas, we can only date this development by means of the all-too-broad chronological parameters of the Aristides scholia more generally, which is to say at some point between the fourth and tenth centuries AD.[181]

Secondly, the development of the term *striglos* would seem to be an essential way-station on the road to the development of the familiar modern-Greek demonic term, *stringlos* (in fact this term would appear to be a synthesis of *striglos* and *strinx*). Like Lamia, this demon too appears as both a singular entity, where Stringlos is its proper name, and as type, where *stringlos* is its category-designation. Though much evolved, the *stringlos* retains some characteristics of its parent *strix*:[182]

a. **Heard not seen.** The *stringlos* is often merely heard, rather than seen. It typically cries out either like a baby, or hoarsely like an animal. However, a normally invisible *stringlos* can be seen by the pure and innocent.

b. **Flying (?).** The path of the unseen creature's sound indicates that it travels at immense speed. It can also be conceptualised as wind or air.

c. **Night-time activity.** The *stringlos* often calls out or attacks by night.

d. **Animal transformation.** It can transform itself into a range of different creatures: cats, dogs, sheep, goats, calves, pigs or donkeys. It also often appears in the form of a human baby, or as a Mischwesen, with a humanoid torso and the lower parts of animal.

e. **Killing.** The *stringlos* can on occasion kill humans by inducing a stroke or a heart-attack. It also kills sheep, by riding on them or by having sex with them. But more often it seems to portend a death – with its cry – rather than to induce one.

---

restored to have said something similar. See Cherubini 2010a: 156–7 nn.40, 45, 46, who accordingly renders Hesychius' phrase 'the space between the wings of an army'.

[180] Schol. Aelius Aristides *Panathenaicus* 102.5 (iii p. 42 Dindorf).

[181] For the dating of the scholia to Aristides, see Dickey 2007: 69.

[182] On all that follows see the remarkable collection of material in the magnificent Blum and Blum 1970, esp. 14 (for the *stringlos* on the bus) and 95–8 (the principal collection of lore); cf. further 50, 65, 76, 118, 124; note also Lawson 1910: 181–4, Patera 2015, esp. 226–8. For some modern Italian folklore reflective of the *strix*-paradigm, see Cherubini 2010a: 30–4, 39–41, 2010b: 67–70. Of particular note is the Sardinian *Surbile* (cf. the Latin adverb *sorbilo*, 'sip by sip'), a woman who transforms herself into a fly to enter houses by invisible means to suck the blood of the new-born; they fail slowly, initially exhibiting only a discoloration (Turchi 1984: 33–45). As to Germanic folklore, one need look no further than *Hansel and Gretel* (no. 15 Grimm).

f. **Protection against.** Methods for protecting against the attack of a *stringlos* include herbal ones, the wearing of amulets made from rue. But amulets can be made from other substances too, incense or the pages of ecclesiastical books. Crucifixes and prayers are also effective. Sheep can be protected by bells.

But in other ways the lore of the *stringlos* can invert the lore of the *strix*, as in a striking tale with a distinctively modern setting. According to this a baby is found in the road by a bus-driver. A nursing mother on his bus offers to give it suck. When it has had its fill the baby speaks out, 'I ate but I did not bite you!', thereby inducing a stroke in the woman. The baby is revealed to be a *stringlos*, with a human head and a serpent body. So here, whereas the *strix* in adult-female form kills or damages the human baby by forcing it to take suck, the *stringlos* in baby form kills the adult-female human by taking milk from her. The *stringlos* in baby form, which often lures victims by presenting itself as a foundling in the road in this way, can be conceptualised as the ghost of, or a demon produced from, a baby that has died unbaptised; it can also be produced when a man rapes the corpse of a dead woman.

We return to the question we set for ourselves at the beginning of this section. The evidence is not decisive, but the probability is that the *strix* was a Roman invention either in fact or in effect, albeit against the background noise of a vigorous international culture of child-killing demons, and that in due course it was appropriated into the Greek tradition.

5 Conclusion

The principal achievement of this *libellus* has been the establishment of the motif-set for what I have called 'the *strix*-paradigm', and the concomitant construction of an idealised *strix* narrative on the basis of it (given at the close of Section 2). The integration of the *strix*-paradigm had a transformative effect, both direct and indirect, on the representation of witches and witchcraft more generally in Latin literature. It is to this paradigm that we should look to explain the radically different feel between Greek and Latin witchcraft narratives, to explain, that is, what I have called 'the gruesome morbidity' of the latter (Section 3). Whilst she fits comfortably into an international culture of child-killing demons, the *strix* is probably best viewed as a Roman creation (Section 4).

Why *did* the *strix* matter? Like the demons Lamia, Gorgo and Mormo, the figure of the *strix* gave body to the anxieties that surrounded infant mortality, and affirmed the importance and value of child-protection. Glib moderns will doubtless tell us that the notion of the *strix*, this horrid, cannibal old woman, evidences a 'misogyny' in Roman society. This could not be further from the truth. She does not tell us to hate women, but rather to admire the care that women invest in the protection of their babies, and to absolve them of blame and indeed to pity them when something goes wrong. Still, it will be complained, the dangerous concept of the *strix* will have led to the torture and execution of innocent elderly women. Perhaps so (although there is no actual evidence of this, for what it is worth) – but how many more innocent young women did the concept protect from the same fate when they lost their babies in circumstances in which no other party was detectably involved? Let us not forget that it is estimated that, prior to the twentieth century, a quarter of all babies died in their first year of life and almost half of all children died before adulthood. One suspects, too, that the *strix* featured more prominently, and with good reason, in the ancient female *imaginaire* than the male one: she was almost certainly a creature of *female discourse* in the first instance.[183]

Why *does* the *strix* matter? The *strix* has bequeathed us, by means direct and indirect, a vital component of the modern popular stereotype of the witch in the Anglo-Saxon west: namely, that she is a hag that flies by night (though of course the *striges* did not need broomsticks to do so).[184] But, as of the mid-nineteenth century, she has bequeathed us a yet stronger legacy, namely, our modern conception of the vampire, this by dint of our Victorian authors combining, in an unfathomable blend, visits to the common well of international folklore with recollections of their Classical educations.[185] The vampires of Bram Stoker's 1897 *Dracula*, to take only the most distinguished example: fly by night, in vespertilian or avian form (Motif B); travel in clouds of dust and penetrate locked rooms through chinks in doors or windows (Motifs D, F), whilst such entry-points are defended against them with the garlic plant or the wild rose (Motif L); drink people's blood (Motif I), in a fashion initially unperceived (Motif J) and gradually destructive (Motif K); and – in the case of the female ones – actually devour babies (Motif G; cf. A, M?).

---

[183] In a conversation with the admirable Dr Heta Björklund in 2017 I expressed regret, from a folklorist's perspective, that we should have been deprived so recently, relatively speaking, of the *living* tradition of the child-killing demon Gello – this after she had flourished in one form or another for perhaps three millennia. I was firmly put in my place: child-killing demons live because babies die, and their passing is hardly to be mourned (cf. Björklund 2017c).
[184] Cf. Cherubini 2010b: 65.   [185] See now Groom 2018.

Abbreviations

BNJ	*Brill's New Jacoby.* 2006– (online resource).
CIL	*Corpus inscriptionum Latinarum.* Berlin 1863–.
CLE	Bücheler *et al.* 1895–1926.
CPG	Leutsch and Schneidewin 1839–51.
FGrH	Jacoby *et al.* 1923–.
ILS	Dessau 1892–1916.
LS	Lewis and Short 1879.
LSJ	Liddell *et al.* 1968.
LIMC	Kahil et al. (1981–99).
MGH	*Monumenta Germaniae historica* (1826).
OLD	Glare 1982.
PG	Migne 1857–1904.
PGM	Preisendanz and Henrichs 1973–4.
PL	Migne 1884–1904.
PMG	Page 1962.
RE	Pauly et al. (1893).
TrGF	Snell *et al.* 1971–2004.

References

Argenti, P. P., and Rose, H. J. (1949). *The Folk-Lore of Chios.* 2 vols. Cambridge: Cambridge University Press.

Banks, S. E., and Binns, J. W., eds. and trans. (2002). *Gervase of Tilbury. Otia Imperialia, Recreation for an Emperor.* Oxford: Oxford University Press.

Beekes, R. (2010). *Etymological Dictionary of Greek.* Leiden: Brill.

Björklund, H. (2017a). Protecting Against Child-Killing Demons. Uterus Amulets in the Late Antique and Byzantine Magical World. Diss., Helsinki. (Subsumes 2017b and 2017c.)

(2017b). Metamorphosis, mixanthropy and the child-killing demon in the Hellenistic and Byzantine periods. *Acta Classica*, 60, 22–49.

(2017c). A note on the aspects of the Greek child-killing demon. *Classica et Mediaevalia*, 66, 341–64.

Blänsdorf, J. (1990). Der Werwolf-Geschichte des Niceros bei Petron als Beispiel literarischer Fiktion mündlichen Erzählens. In G. Vogt-Spira ed. *Strukturen der Mündlichkeit in der römischen Literatur.* Tübingen: Narr, pp. 193–217.

Blum, R., and Blum, E. (1970). *The Dangerous Hour. The Lore and Culture of Crisis and Mystery in Rural Greece.* London: Chatto & Windus.

Boardman, J. (1992). Lamia. In *LIMC* vi.1, p.189.

Boehm, F. (1931). Striges. In *RE* 2 Reihe 4.1, pp. 356–63.

Bolton, J. D. P. (1962). *Aristeas of Proconessus.* Oxford: Oxford University Press.

Bömer, F. (1958–63). *P. Ovidius Naso. Die Fasten.* 2 vols. Heidelberg: Winter.

Boyce, B. (1991). *The Language of the Freedmen in Petronius' 'Cena Trimalchionis'.* Leiden: Brill.

Bremmer, J. N. (1998). The novel and the apocryphal Acts. Place, time and readership. In H. Hofmann and M. Zimmerman eds. *Groningen Colloquia on the Novel ix.* Groningen: Forsten, pp. 157–80.

(2016). Shamanism in Classical scholarship. Where are we now? In P. Jackson ed. *Horizons of Shamanism. A Triangular Approach.* Stockholm Studies in Comparative Religion 35. Stockholm: Stockholm University Press, pp. 52–78.

Brodersen, K., ed. and trans. (2016). *Quintus Serenus, Medizinischer Rat (Liber medicinalis).* Berlin: De Gruyter.

Bücheler, F., Riese, A., and Lommatzsch, E. (1895–1926). *Anthologia Latina.* ii. *Carmina latina epigraphica.* 3 vols. Leipzig: Teubner.

Burkert, W. (1962). Goes. Zum griechischen Schamanismus. *Rheinisches Museum* 105, 36–55. Reprinted in Burkert 2001–11: iii, pp. 173–90.

(1972). *Lore and Science in Ancient Pythagoreanism*. Cambridge, MA: Harvard University Press.

(1992). *The Orientalizing Revolution. Near-Eastern Influence on Greek Culture in the Early Archaic Age*. Cambridge, MA: Harvard University Press. Translation of *Die orientalisierende Epoche in der griechischen Religion und Literatur*. Heidelberg: Winter, 1984.

(2001–11). *Kleine Schriften*. 8 vols. Göttingen: Vandenhoeck & Ruprecht.

Celoria, F. (1992). *The Metamorphoses of Antoninus Liberalis*. London: Routledge.

Chantraine, P. (2008). *Dictionnaire étymologique de la langue grecque. Histoire des mots*. 2nd ed. Paris: Klinksieck.

Cherubini, L. (2009a). *Scilicet illum tetigerat mala manus*. Inganni e disinganni delle streghe in Petr. 63. *I quaderni del ramo d'oro*, 2, 143–55.

(2009b). The virgin, the bear, the upside-down *strix*. An interpretation of Antoninus Liberalis 21. *Arethusa*, 42, 77–97.

(2010a). *Strix. La strega nella cultura romana*. Turin: UTET libreria.

(2010b). Hungry witches and children in Antiquity and the Middle Ages. In K. Mustakallio and C. Laes eds. *The Dark Side of Childhood in Late Antiquity and the Middle Ages*. Oxford: Oxbow, pp. 67–78.

Curletto, S. (1987). Il contesto mitico-religioso antenato/anima/uccello/strega nel mondo greco-latino. *Maia*, 39, 143–56.

Dench, E. (1995). *From Barbarians to New Men. Greek, Roman, and Modern Perceptions of Peoples from the Central Apennines*. Oxford: Oxford University Press.

Dessau, H. (1892–1916). *Inscriptiones Latinae selectae*. 3 vols. Berlin: Weidmann.

De Vaan, M. A. C. (2008). *Etymological Dictionary of Latin and the Other Italic Languages*. Leiden: Brill.

Dickey, E. (2007). *Ancient Greek Scholarship*. New York: American Philological Association.

Dickie, M. W. (2001). *Magic and Magicians in the Graeco-Roman World*. London: Routledge.

Drew, K. F. (1991). *The Laws of the Salian Franks*. Philadelphia: Pennsylvania University Press.

Duckworth, G. E. (1952). *The Nature of Roman Comedy*. Princeton: Princeton University Press.

Eidinow, E. (2018). 'The horror of the terrifying and the hilarity of the grotesque'. Daimonic spaces – and emotions – in ancient Greek literature. *Arethusa*, 51, 209–35.

Elliott, J. H. (2015–17). *Beware the Evil Eye*. 4 vols. Eugene, OR: Cascade.

Ernout, A., and Meillet, A. (1959). *Dictionnaire étymologique de la langue latine*. 4th ed. Paris: Klincksieck.

Farber, W. (1983). Lamaštu. In *Reallexikon der Assyriologie* 6, 439–46. Berlin: Walter de Gruyter.

(1989). *Schlaf, Kindchen, Schlaf! Mesopotamische Baby-Beschworungen und -Rituale*. Winona Lake, IN: Eisenbrauns.

Frangoulidis, S. (2008). *Witches, Isis and Narrative. Approaches to Magic in Apuleius' Metamorphoses*. Berlin: De Gruyter.

Frankfurter, D. (2014). The social context of women's erotic magic in Antiquity. In K. B. Stratton and D. S. Kalleres eds. *Daughters of Hecate. Women and Magic in the Ancient World*. Oxford: Oxford University Press, pp. 319–33.

Frazer, Sir James G. (1929). *The Fasti of Ovid*. 5 vols. London: Macmillan.

Friedlaender, L. ed. and trans. (1906). *Petroni* Cena Trimalchionis. Leipzig: S. Hirzel.

Frisk, H. (1960–72). *Griechisches etymologisches Wörterbuch*. 3 vols. Heidelberg: Winter.

Gaide, F. (1995). Les histories du loup-garou et des *striges* dans la *Cena Trimalchionis* ou la narration du 'vécu'. Deux joyaux du Latin vulgaire. In L. Callebat ed. *Latin vulgaire – Latin tardif.* iv. Hildesheim: Olms, pp. 715–23.

Gaster, M. (1900). Two thousand years of a charm against the child-stealing witch. *Folklore*, 11, 129–62.

Glare, P. G. W., ed. (1982). *Oxford Latin Dictionary*. Oxford: Oxford University Press.

Gordon, R. L. (1987). Lucan's Erictho. In M. Whitby, P. Hardie and M. Whitby eds. *Homo viator. Classical Essays for John Bramble*. Bristol: Bristol Classical Press, pp. 231–41.

(1999). Imagining Greek and Roman magic. In V. Flint, R. L. Gordon, G. Luck and D. Ogden *Witchcraft and Magic in Europe*. ii. *Ancient Greece and Rome*. London: Athlone, pp. 159–75.

Green, R. F. (2016). *Elf Queens and Holy Friars. Fairy Beliefs in the Medieval Church*. Philadelphia: University of Pennsylvania Press.

Greenfield, R. P. H. (1988). *Traditions of Belief in Late Byzantine Demonology*. Amsterdam: Hakkert.

Grimm, Brüder (1986). *Kinder- und Hausmärchen, gesammelt durch die Brüder Grimm*. 3 vols. Göttingen: Vandenhoeck & Ruprecht. [The standard edition of the original 1812–15 work.]

Groom, N. (2018). *The Vampire. A New History*. New Haven: Yale University Press.

Haavio, M. (1958). Der Seelenvogel. *Studia Fennica*, 8, 61–81.

Halleux, R., and Schamp, J. (1985). *Les Lapidaires grecs*. Paris: Les Belles Lettres.

Hansen, P. A., ed. (2005). *Hesychii Alexandrini lexicon*. iii. Berlin: De Gruyter.

Hansen, W. F. (1996). *Phlegon of Tralles' Book of Marvels*. Exeter: Exeter University Press.

Heyworth, S. J. (2007). *Cynthia: A Companion to the Text of Propertius*. Oxford: Oxford University Press.

Hill, D. E. (1973). The Thessalian trick. *Rheinisches Museum* 116, 221–38.

Hofstetter, E. (1997). Seirenes. In *LIMC* viii.1, pp. 1093–104.

Hordern, J. H. (2004). *Sophron's Mimes*. Oxford: Oxford University Press.

Hutchinson, G. O., ed. (2006). *Properties. Elegies, Book IV*. Cambridge: Oxford University Press.

Hutton, R. (2017). *The Witch. A History of Fear, from Ancient Times to the Present*. New Haven: Yale University Press.

Hutton, W. (2005). *Describing Greece. Landscape and Literature in the Periegesis of Pausanias*. Cambridge: Cambridge University Press.

Ingemark, C. A., and Ingemark, D. (2013). More than scapegoating. The therapeutic potential of stories of child-killing demons in ancient Greece and Rome. In C. A. Ingemark ed. *Therapeutic Uses of Storytelling. An Interdisciplinary Approach to Narration as Therapy*. Lund: Nordic Academic Press, pp. 75–84.

Jacoby, F. *et al.*, eds. (1923–). *Die Fragmente der griechischen Historiker*. Multiple volumes and parts. Berlin and Leiden: Weidmann, Brill.

James, M. R., Brooke, C. N. L., and Mynors, R. A. B., eds. (1983). *Walter Map. De Nugis Curialium. Courtiers' Trifles*. Oxford: Oxford University Press.

Johnston, S. I. (1995). Defining the dreadful. Remarks on the Greek child-killing demon. In M. Meyer and P. Mirecki eds. *Ancient Magic and Ritual Power*. Leiden: Brill, pp. 361–87.

(1999). *Restless Dead. Encounters Between the Living and the Dead in Ancient Greece*. Berkeley: University of California Press.

Kahil, L., *et al.*, eds. (1981–99). *Lexicon Iconographicum Mythologiae Classicae*. 9 vols. Zurich and Munich: Artemis.

(1988). Harpyiai. In *LIMC* iv.1, pp.445–50.

Keil, H., ed. (1855–1923). *Grammatici Latini*. 8 vols. Leipzig: Teubner.

Keulen, W. H. (2007). *Apuleius Madaurensis Metamorphoses, Book I. Text, Introduction and Commentary*. Leiden: Brill.

Kieckhefer, R. (1998). Avenging the blood of children. Anxiety over child victims and the origins of the European witch trials. In A. Ferreiro ed. *The Devil, Heresy and Witchcraft in the Middle Ages. Essays in Honor of Jeffrey B. Russell*. Leiden: Brill, pp. 91–109.

Korenjak, M. (1996). *Die Ericthoszene in Lukans Pharsalia. Einleitung, Text, Übersetzung, Kommentar.* Frankfurt am Main: Lang.

Laistner, M., ed. (1926). *Philoxeni Glossarium.* Glossaria Latina ii. Paris: Les Belles Lettres.

Lattimore, R. (1942). *Themes in Greek and Latin Epitaphs.* Urbana: Illinois University Press.

Lawson, J. C. (1910). *Modern Greek Folklore and Ancient Greek Religion.* Cambridge: Cambridge University Press.

Leinweber, D. W. (1994). Witchcraft and lamiae in 'The Golden Ass'. *Folklore,* 105, 77–82.

Letta, C. (1972). *I Marsi e il Fucino nell'antichità.* Milan: Cisalpino-Goliardica.

Leutsch, E. L. von., and Schneidewin, F. G. (1839–51). *Corpus paroemiographorum Graecorum.* 2 vols. Göttingen: Vanderhoeck & Ruprecht.

Lewis, C. T., and Short, C., eds. (1879). *A Latin Dictionary.* Oxford: Oxford University Press.

Liddell, H. G., Scott, R., and Jones, H.S., eds. (1968). *A Greek–English Lexicon.* 9th ed. with supplement. Oxford: Oxford University Press.

Litavrin, G. G. (2003). *Кекавмен, Советы и Рассказы.* 2nd ed. St Petersburg: Aleteia.

Littlewood, R. J. (2006). *A Commentary on Ovid Fasti, Book* VI. Oxford: Oxford University Press.

McDonough, C. (1997). Carna, Proca and the *strix* on the Kalends of June. *TAPA,* 127, 315–44.

McKeown, J. C. (1989). *Ovid. Amores. Text, Prolegomena and Commentary.* Leeds: Cairns.

Maltby, R. (1990). *A Lexicon of Ancient Latin Etymologies.* ARCA. Leeds: Cairns.

Mancini, L. (2005). *Il rovinoso incanto. Storie di sirene antiche.* Bologna: Il mulino.

Marinatos, N. (2000). *The Goddess and the Warrior. The Naked Goddess and the Mistress of Animals in Early Greek Religion.* London: Routledge.

Marshall, P. K., ed. (2002). *Hygini Fabulae.* 2nd ed. Stuttgart: Teubner.

Migne, J. P., ed. (1857–1904). *Patrologiae cursus completus. Series Graeca.* Paris: Garnier.

(1884–1904). *Patrologiae cursus completus. Series Latina.* Paris: Garnier.

Monumenta Germaniae historica (1826–). Hannover: Hahn.

Ogden, D. (2001). *Greek and Roman Necromancy.* Princeton: Princeton University Press.

(2007). *In Search of the Sorcerer's Apprentice. The Traditional Tales of Lucian's Lover of Lies.* Swansea: Classical Press of Wales.

(2008). *Night's Black Agents.* London: Continuum.

(2009). *Magic, Witchcraft and Ghosts in the Greek and Roman Worlds. A Sourcebook.* 2nd ed. New York: Oxford University Press USA.

(2013). *Drakōn. Dragon Myth and Serpent Cult in the Greek and Roman Worlds.* Oxford: Oxford University Press.

(2018). John Damascene on dragons and witches. Translation and select commentary. *Pegasus*, 60, 16–25.

(2021). *The Werewolf in the Ancient World.* Oxford: Oxford University Press.

(forthcoming). *The Dragon in the West.* Oxford: Oxford University Press.

Oliphant, S. G. (1913). The story of the *strix*. Ancient. *TAPA*, 44, 133–49.

(1914). The story of the *strix*. Isidorus and the glossographers. *TAPA*, 44, 49–63.

Page, D. L., ed. (1962). *Poetae melici Graeci.* Oxford: Oxford University Press.

Papathomopoulos, M. (2002). *Antoninus Liberalis. Les Métamorphoses.* Paris: Les Belles Lettres.

Patera, M. (2015). *Figures grecques de l'épouvante de l'antiquité au present. Peurs enfantines et adultes.* Mnemosyne Suppl. 376. Leiden: Brill.

Paule, M. T. (2017). *Canidia, Rome's First Witch.* London: Bloomsbury.

Pauly, A., Wissowa, G., and Kroll, W., eds. (1893–). *Realencyclopädie der klassischen Altertumswissenschaft.* Multiple volumes and parts. Munich: Metzler.

Pettazzoni, R. (1940). Carna. *Studi Etruschi*, 14, 163–72.

Phillips, J. H. (1991). *Liber medicinalis Quinti Sereni* 58, 1029–1030. Teething pain and a terminus post quem. In P. Defosse ed. *Hommages à Carl Deroux* ii. *Prose et linguistique, médecine.* Brussels: Latomus, pp. 557–60.

Polites, N. G. (1871). Μελέτη ἐπὶ τοῦ βίου τῶν νεωτερῶν Ἑλλήνων. Athens: Naki and Wilberg.

Preisendanz, K., and Henrichs, A. (1973–4). *Papyri Graecae Magicae. Die griechischen Zauberpapyri.* 2nd ed. 2 vols. Stuttgart: Teubner.

Resnick, I. M., and Kitchell, K. F., Jr. (2007). 'The sweepings of Lamia'. Transformations of the myths of Lilith and Lamia. In A. Cuffel and B. Britt eds. *Religion, Gender, and Culture in the Pre-Modern World.* Basingstoke: Palgrave, pp. 77–104.

Ribbeck, O. (1873). *Comicorum Romanorum praeter Plautum et Terentium fragmenta.* Leipzig: Teubner.

Rose, K. F. C. (1971). *The Date and Author of the Satyricon.* Leiden: Brill.

Schmeling, G. L. (2011). *A Commentary on the Satyrica of Petronius.* Oxford: Oxford University Press.

Schuster, M. (1930). Der Werwolf und die Hexen. *WS*, 48, 149–78.

Scobie, A. S. (1975). *Apuleius 'Metamorphoses' (Asinus aureus)* i. *A Commentary.* Meisenheim am Glan: Hain.

(1978). Strigiform witches in Roman and other cultures. *Fabula*, 19, 74–101.

(1983). *Apuleius and Folklore: Toward a History of ML3045, AaTh567, 449A*. London: Folklore Society.

Smith, M. S. (1975). *Petronius. Cena Trimalchionis*. Oxford: Oxford University Press.

Snell, B., Kannicht, R., and Radt, S. (1971–2004). *Tragicorum Graecorum fragmenta*. 5 vols. Göttingen: Vanderhoeck & Ruprecht.

Spaeth, B. S. (2010). 'The terror that comes in the night'. The night hag and supernatural assault in Latin literature. In E. Schioli and C. Walde eds. *Sub imagine somni. Nighttime Phenomena in Greco-Roman Culture*. Pisa: ETS, pp. 231–58.

Spier, J. (1993). Medieval Byzantine amulets and their tradition. *Journal of the Warburg and Courtauld Institutes*, 56, 25–62.

Stoker, B. (1897). *Dracula*. London: Constable.

Thompson, S. (1955–8). *Motif-Index of Folk-Literature*. 2nd ed. 6 vols. Bloomington: Indiana University Press.

Touati, C. (2003). Des striges antiques aux sorcières médiévales. Mémoire de Licence, Université de Neuchâtel. [*Non vidi.*]

Tupet, A.-M. (1976). *La magie dans la poésie latine*. i. *Des origins à la fin du règne d'Auguste*. Paris: Les Belles Lettres.

(1986). Rites magiques dans l'antiquité romaine. In *ANRW*, ii.16.3, 2591–675.

Turchi D. (1984). *Leggende e racconti popolari della Sardegna*. Rome: Newton Compton.

Ustinova, Y. (2009). *Caves and the Early Greek Mind*. Oxford: Oxford University Press.

Väänänen, V. (1967). *Introduction au latin vulgaire*. 2nd ed. Paris: Klincksiek.

Van der Paardt, R. T. (1971). *Apuleius. The Metamorphoses III*. Amsterdam: Hakkert.

Van Mal-Maeder, D. (2001). *Apuleius Madaurensis Metamorphoses, Livre II*. Groningen: Forsten.

Viltanioti, I. F. (2012). La Démone Yellô dans la Grèce ancienne, byzantine et modern. In J. Ries and H. Limet eds. *Anges et démons*. Louvain-la-Neuve: Centre d'Histoire des Religions, pp. 173–89.

Vollmer, F., ed. (1916). *Quinti Sereni, Liber medicinalis*. CML ii.3. Leipzig: Teubner.

Watson, L. C. (2003). *A Commentary on Horace's 'Epodes'*. Oxford: Oxford University Press.

(2019). *Magic in Ancient Greece and Rome*. London: Bloomsbury.

West, D. R. (1991). Gello and Lamia. Two Hellenic daimons of Semitic origin. *Ugarit-Forschungen*, 23, 361–68.

(1995). *Some Cults of the Greek Goddesses and Female Daemons of Oriental Origin*. Alter Orient und Altes Testament 233. Neukirchen-Vlyun: Neukirchener Verlag.

Wiggermann, F. A. M. (2000). X. Lamaštu, daughter of Anu, a profile. In M. Stol and F. A. M. Wiggermann *Birth in Babylonia and the Bible. Its Mediterranean Setting*. Groningen: Styx, pp. 217–53.

Wolohojian, A. M., trans. (1969). *The Romance of Alexander the Great by Pseudo-Callisthenes. Translated from the Armenian Version*. New York: Columbia University Press.

Yarnall, J. (1994). *Transformations of Circe. History of an Enchantress*. Urbana: Illinois University Press.

わが最愛の妻
江里子に

Cambridge Elements ☰

Magic

Marion Gibson
University of Exeter
Marion Gibson is Professor of Renaissance and Magical Literatures and Director of the
Flexible Combined Honours Programme at the University of Exeter. Her publications
include *Possession, Puritanism and Print: Darrell, Harsnett, Shakespeare and the Elizabethan
Exorcism Controversy* (2006), *Witchcraft Myths in American Culture* (2007), *Imagining the
Pagan Past: Gods and Goddesses in Literature and History since the Dark Ages* (2013), *The
Arden Shakespeare Dictionary of Shakespeare's Demonology* (with Jo Esra, 2014),
Rediscovering Renaissance Witchcraft (2017) and *Witchcraft: The Basics* (2018). Her new
book, *The Witches of St Osyth: Persecution, Murder and Betrayal in Elizabethan England*, will
be published by CUP in 2022.

About the Series
Elements in Magic aims to restore the study of magic, broadly defined, to a central place
within culture: one which it occupied for many centuries before being set apart by
changing discourses of rationality and meaning. Understood as a continuing and potent
force within global civilisation, magical thinking is imaginatively approached here as
a cluster of activities, attitudes, beliefs and motivations which include topics such as
alchemy, astrology, divination, exorcism, the fantastical, folklore, haunting, supernatural
creatures, necromancy, ritual, spirit possession and witchcraft.

Cambridge Elements ≡

Magic

Elements in the Series

The Strix-*Witch*
Daniel Ogden

A full series listing is available at: www.cambridge.org/EMGI

Printed in the United States
by Baker & Taylor Publisher Services